Flower Child

Brenda Eldridge

Flower Child

The heart of a flower child will thrive anywhere

for Ella Grace

Flower Child
ISBN 978 1 76109 168 1
Copyright © text and illustrations Brenda Eldridge 2021
Cover painting: *Queen of the Hedgerows*, Brenda Eldridge

First published 2021 by
Ginninderra Press
PO Box 3461 Port Adelaide 5015
www.ginninderrapress.com.au

Contents

Hyacinth	7
Pheasant-eye Narcissus	12
Campion and Bluebell	16
Dog Rose	19
Honeysuckle	24
Queen Anne's Lace	29
Traveller's Joy or Old Man's Beard	35
White Daisy	41
Fuchsia	46
Poppy	52
Calendula	60
Horse Chestnut	66
Mistletoe	71
Snowdrops	76

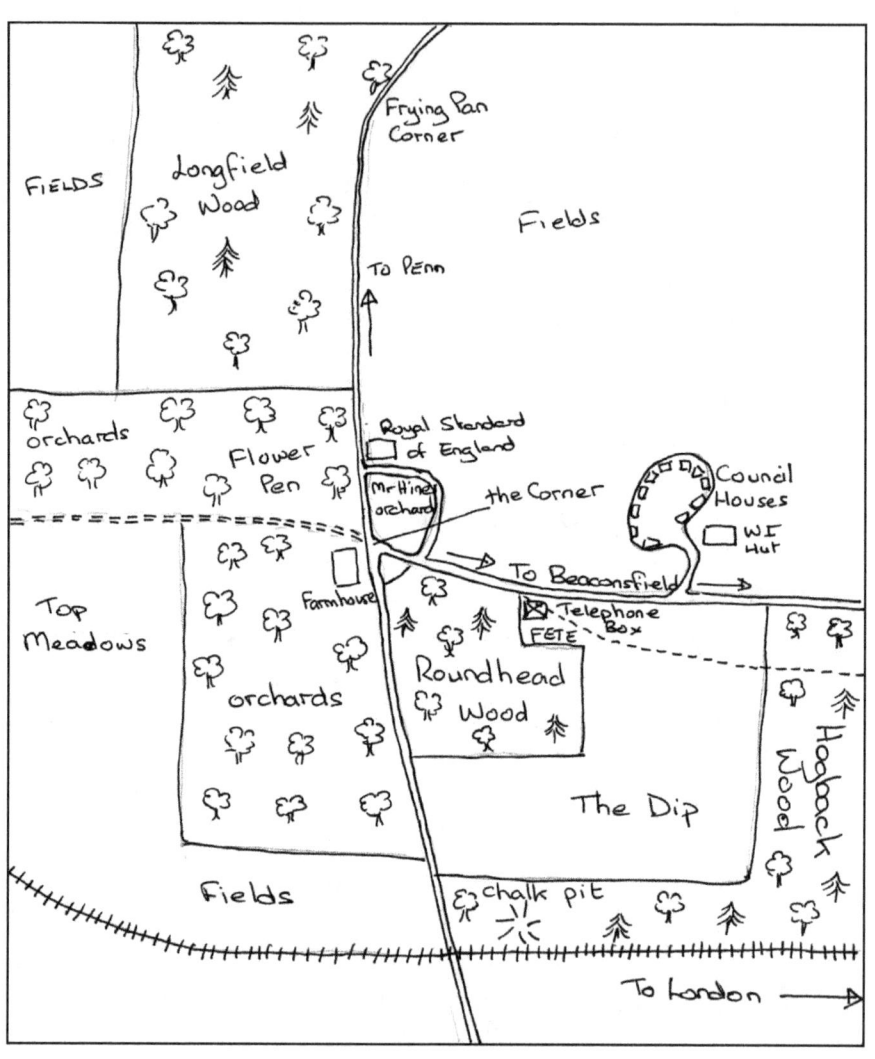

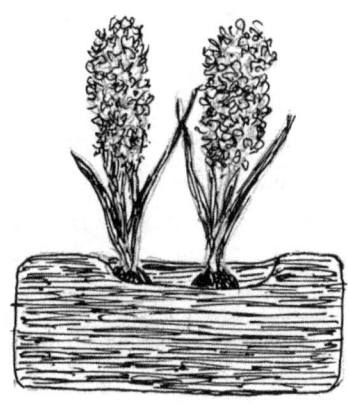

Hyacinth
Hyacinthus orientalis

Mid-afternoon in the kitchen washing dishes and half-watching sun sparkles on the tidal reach outside the window, I became aware of the distinctive sweet perfume of a hyacinth and tumbled back more than sixty years to the old English farmhouse where I grew up.

Mother had a ceramic planter shaped like a hollow log about twelve inches long. Sometime in late autumn, I would be sent off to Roundhead Wood, a beechwood across the lane, with a small bucket and trowel. My task was to bring home leaf mould. I'm not sure how many adults, never mind children, would know these days what I'm talking about.

Among the beech trees grew a few big holly bushes and it was under them where the beech leaves seemed to gather. In these sheltered places, old leaves decayed and broke down to become leaf mould.

I would carefully move aside the drier leaves – watching out for the fallen holly leaves with their sharp spikes – until I found the rich moist mould beneath. Taking out the twiggy bits, I carefully put the darkest coloured earthy mould in my bucket and pushed the dry leaves back to cover the place I had been.

Once home again, under instructions from Mother, I half-filled the log, placed two hyacinth bulbs in – yes, making sure they were the right way up – and covering them. It felt like tucking them up in bed.

Today's children know about 'the cupboard under the stairs' from the Harry Potter books and movies. Our cupboard under the stairs was used to keep firewood and the floor of it was covered in old wood and bark chippings – looking much like the mulch we now buy from the garden centre.

We lived in the heart of the countryside in the Chiltern Hills, about halfway between London and Oxford. The village of Forty Green was surrounded by beechwoods, meadows and orchards. All year, my dad kept a look out for fallen branches and old broken fenceposts and brought them home and piled them in the orchard beside the garden fence. Throughout autumn, winter and spring, every Saturday afternoon, my two older brothers, Steve and Geoff, and I helped Dad saw this store of wood into logs then split them with an axe. I can still hear my dad's voice telling me to pull the bow saw not to push it. The logs had then to be carried indoors and placed in the cupboard under the stairs which was next to the open fireplace.

We all complained of cold hands when the logs still had snow on them or it was raining, and the old saying about the wood keeping us warm twice – once when working hard sawing and chopping and again when we sat by the fire – was small comfort. We threw the logs into the back of the cupboard any old how but carefully stacked them tidily at the front. We also had to watch out for spiders and mice – it was an ideal place for them all year.

Mother's ceramic log of hyacinth bulbs was placed in a corner of the wood cupboard where it was dark and kept warm by the fire. Around Christmas, the bulbs sent up thick dark green leaves and the central stem of buds. Only then was it brought out into the sitting room. I remember the anticipation, waiting to see if the flowers would be pink, blue or white. Pink and blue were my favourites but they all smelled the same. They were a wonderful splash of colour in our dim, low-ceilinged sitting room with its heavy support beams and small windows.

The farmhouse was actually two adjoining cottages that had been knocked into one by means of a kitchen being built on the back giving access to both sides of the house. There were two front doors and a back door into the kitchen. There was a spiral staircase going round a chimney stack at each end of the house, so of course there were two cupboards under the stairs. The third chimney stack was for the combustion stove in the kitchen lit on Saturdays to heat the water for baths.

When I was young, we used the sitting room with the red flagstoned floor. It had a large window that faced north beside the front door that could be opened but wasn't used much and a smaller window that faced south. Above it was my parents' bedroom. There was a small addition – less than ten feet square – on to the north wall that downstairs was used as a walk-in pantry and upstairs as my bedroom. Facing north with three outside walls and two small windows, my bedroom was always cold. I can recall ice crackling on the eiderdown where my breath had made it damp overnight.

Following the birth of my youngest brother, we began using what had been the spare room as our sitting room, and the old sitting room became the spare room. This room was much warmer, as it had a wooden floor. In those days, babies were mostly born at home and my parents' bed was dismantled and brought downstairs and put in the spare room. This way, for the week or so after the birth, Mother was able to stay in bed to recover and still keep an eye on her family. The second front door that would have opened into this room had been boarded up and plastered over.

Above this sitting room was my brothers' bedroom, and the bathroom and airing cupboard were above the kitchen. I don't remember the airing cupboard being used for anything except to house the hot water tank. Other than Saturdays, kettles had to be boiled for hot water. This seemed to take ages when waiting to have a turn in the tin bath. There was something cosy about sitting in warm water in front of an open fire.

The reality was that there were also cold draughts coming in through the many gaps in doors and windows in the old farmhouse, so the side of me that faced the fire was too warm, while the rest of me shivered.

Mother didn't have a washing machine either in those days and had a gas-heated copper to wash everything in. There was a smooth copper stick, a shortened broom handle, for lifting the hot clothes up and put through the rollers to squeeze out the water and dropped into the sink for rinsing. They were dangerous times when compared with the ease of today's washing machines and clothes dryers.

We had a washing line attached to the downpipe beside the back door and a pole fixed to the fence across the garden. The clothes, towels and sheets were pegged out and a clothes prop used to keep them off the ground. The prop was a long strong stick from a sapling with a V shape at the top where the washing line sat. It was a terrible thing when strong winds or just wear and tear broke the line and the washing would be dragged over the dirt and had to be washed again.

We had no electricity until a short time before my youngest brother was born in 1961. This meant Mother had to use the old flat irons. There were two; one was heating on the gas stove while the other was used to iron clothes and sheets as quickly as possible before the heat faded. We had gas lighting and we lit our way up the stairs for bed with candles. The lights made a wonderful soft pop when lit and the filament glowed red briefly when turned off.

We had gas for cooking and I remember the gas meter in a cupboard under the sink. Coins to feed the meter had to be kept on hand – such a to-do if the gas ran out halfway through a meal being prepared or a cake baked. The gas man came probably every six months to read the meter, take out the coins to pay for the gas used and refund the balance. I was fascinated as he counted the pennies, threepenny pieces and later on shillings, into neat piles. Money was something that was hard come by and had to be spent carefully. This little bonus of refunded coins was such a treat. Did it go towards new clothes or shoes, some household appliance or was it fed back into the meter straightaway? I don't know.

There was another aspect to the gas. This was in the days before natural gas. The gas of those times polluted the air we breathed and was deadly if there was a leak. It also made it very difficult to grow indoor plants, which takes me back to the magic of the hyacinths flowering for such a brief period.

I can remember being given a special glass vase which I filled with water and a hyacinth bulb placed in the bowl shape at the top. This too was placed in the wood cupboard until the leaves appeared and I loved to watch how the white roots grew and filled the lower part of the vase at the same time as the stem was growing upwards.

I have one of these glasses now on the bench in our kitchen. It is a pink hyacinth that, as yet, only has two buds opening but their perfume was enough to send me off into the world of my childhood.

Pheasant-eye Narcissus
Narcissus poeticus

As a child, I didn't know anything about the ancient Greek mythologies. I was in my mid-thirties before I learned about the story of Narcissus, who turned into the flower that I knew from childhood as pheasant-eye narcissus.

To see and smell a narcissus anytime immediately transports me back to an orchard called the Flower Pen. Only a few paces from home, I stepped into an enchanted world. Where to begin to describe it?

If I close my eyes, I can walk across the farmyard skirting around the muddy puddles left by spring showers, out onto the unsurfaced lane. The banks below Mr Perfect's hedge were a mass of rich green rounded leaves and starred with golden yellow lesser celandines and deep mauve violets. The celandines only opened in the sun and closed quickly when it became shadowed. Their petals were narrower than the round petals of buttercups but they gleamed the same as if covered in clear varnish.

In times before my childhood, girls from a young age were employed as maids in the nearby manor houses. Once a year, they were allowed to go and visit their mothers – hence it came to be called

Mothering Sunday – and they usually took a small gift. Those days and customs are long gone, but I always gave Mother a posy of celandines and violets on Mothering Sunday.

Clambering over the wooden fence into the Flower Pen, I had to watch out for stinging nettles and long wet grass. I could hear songbirds – blackbirds, thrushes, robins, wrens – and the homely chirp of sparrows and countless other birds I knew by sight but perhaps not by their song. I admired the tiny ones like the blue tits who were so fierce if I sat on a fallen log for a picnic lunch and too close to where they had built a nest.

Overhead, a sky deepest blue after winter's paleness, with scatterings of billowing white clouds which could bring an unexpected and unwelcome shower.

The apple trees were laid out in straight rows. They were old and gnarled but someone had shaped them to look like umbrellas – at least to my eyes. They were a mass of pink and white blossom. My instinct was always to pick a stem or two just to be able to take them home and savour each blossom with its petals darker pink on the outside and almost white inside. But growing up on a farm, we learned early the harsh practical aspects of life. If I wanted apples to eat at the end of summer, then I had to leave the blossom on the bough…

The farm didn't belong to my parents. My dad was employed by a wealthy property developer as an agricultural worker and he preferred mechanics and growing crops to animal husbandry. During World War II, he worked for the Ministry of Agriculture as one of the mechanics keeping the farm equipment in working order for the Land Army girls. It was where he met my mother. When the war ended, he was considered fortunate to find a job that provided a cottage for him to live in. The downside was, if he left the job, he and his family would be homeless. There were many times when I'm sure he wanted to leave (I heard he wanted to come to Australia) but with a young family there was little choice but to stay on.

It was even more disheartening for him that the farm was run at a loss for some kind of tax benefit and I think this drained my dad of any enthusiasm for his job. Every morning from Monday to Saturday, he trudged round to the field called the Dip where the phone box stood, and rang his boss for instructions for the day. How soul-destroying that must have been for him, though I didn't think of it at all at the time – it was just something that Dad always did – that, and making sure he had the four pennies required to make the call.

But back to the Flower Pen. Wordsworth wrote of a host of golden daffodils. We had a host of pheasant-eye narcissus growing between the apple trees. They were grown by the boss's sister Mary for selling at market along with some King Alfred daffodils – they had large trumpets slightly darker yellow than the outer petals.

We earned money by picking the flowers, making sure they were plucked where the stem was green not the white part at the base, and tying them into bunches of six with raffia with all the blooms facing the same way. It was a messy job, as anyone who has picked daffodils or narcissus can tell you. They have thick sticky slimy stuff in the stems that went all over your hands and clothes as soon as you broke the stem.

Mary was a cheerful kindly person as I remember her. She would come to collect the boxes of flowers and provide fruit cake and flasks of tea for lunch. Because I was and always will be a flower child at heart, I was delighted when I was allowed to keep some of the shorter-stemmed blooms to take home to Mother. I searched the hedgerows for bluebells and white campion and a sprig of beech leaves and presented them to her to put in the one old crystal vase we had. It was there I noticed that wild flowers really don't like being indoors and they drooped quickly and were dead by the next morning.

Why were we keen to earn some pocket money? To go to the fair of course.

Beaconsfield Old Town was about three miles from the farmhouse. It had grown up around a crossroads that was partly formed by the main A40 road between London and Oxford. Every year on 10 May, there was the fair. Records show that the fair has been held since 1239 and

Lesser celandine
Ficaria verna

Violet or dog violet
Viola riviniana

hadn't missed a year since, even during the war years, although the lights were kept off then. By the time we knew it, it was sideshows, merry-go-rounds and stalls to buy toffee apples and candyfloss. In earlier times, it was more for agriculture – the buying and selling of stock and employment opportunities for those in need of work.

The coconut shies were a dazzlement. My dad and brothers would throw a wooden ball the size of a cricket ball at coconuts held in a shallow dish on a stick. If you knocked the coconut off, it was yours – not as easy as you might think. At home, we had the horrible task of knocking a hole in the nut with a hammer and nail to drain off the milk, then trying to get the shell from the meat. Again the hammer was called into use. The shells were very hard and I often wondered if it was really worth all the effort.

One of the last vestiges of the old days were the Morris dancers. I didn't know it then, but some research tells me that Morris dancing goes back to the fifteenth century and varies in different parts of England. It's the rhythmic stepping of choreographed figures by a group of dancers usually wearing ribbons and pads on their shins. It's a sort of mock fight using sticks, swords and handkerchiefs to the accompaniment of accordions, drums and/or fiddles. Another character called the Fool rode a hobby horse and carried an inflated pig's bladder attached to a stick. Any dancer not performing properly was hit with the pig's bladder.

Campion and Bluebell
Silene dioica and *Hyacinthoides hispanica*

Rudyard Kipling wrote in his poem 'In Springtime', 'Give me back one day in England, for it's Spring in England now…'

I always misquote it – 'Oh to be in England now that spring is there…' – but the message is the same. There is nowhere in the world quite like England in spring and for me spring and England are forever synonymous with bluebells. I have grown them here in my garden in Australia. They look the same and smell the same but they aren't growing in beechwoods…

Forty Green was not really a village. We had no village green or pond, no street lighting and no church, though we did have a public house. Forty Green was a hamlet. The map on page 6 shows the layout of Forty Green as I remember it but some of the old lanes have been renamed and I don't know if the fields are still referred to by the same names as I knew them. The farmhouse stood at a junction always referred to as the Corner. Riding Lane was once a Roman road between Holtspur on the A40 and the village of Penn and was about three miles long. Forty Green was halfway between the two villages. Another road came in to connect at the Corner and took us to our closest town of Beaconsfield.

I can remember when Riding Lane was unsurfaced – just a dirt track. Even the road to Beaconsfield was unsurfaced until a small council estate was built at the far end of the village in the late 1950s. It was such fun to burst the bubbles of black tarmac that appeared on hot summer days, though I can remember Mother lamenting that the black on our socks didn't wash out.

All directions were given to go to the Corner and turn left or right et cetera. I remember seeing photographs of my youngest brother long after I left the village. He built a snowman on the bank by the Corner as tall as he was to impress the girl who could see it from her bedroom window. As soon as he built it, there came a hard frost and the story goes it stood there for weeks and directions changed to 'Go to the snowman and turn left or right...'

To get into Roundhead Wood, I went down a set of steps cut into the bank (about three metres high) in front of the farmhouse, walked perhaps fifty metres down Riding Lane and then climbed up another bank into the wood which was level with the farmhouse and the orchards at the end of the garden.

Bluebells grew in the shade of the copper beeches. There were masses of them on the far side of the wood. They even crept out into the Dip. It wasn't just the bluebells that called me. Oh yes, they were a magic carpet of blue and mauve – I could have sworn I could hear their tiny bells chiming – but it was the new beech leaves that set them off to perfection. There is a particular shade of pale green I have only ever seen in new beech leaves. They are so delicate covering twigs on lower branches and, although called copper beeches for the colour their leaves turn in autumn, their trunks were tall, straight and had silver bark. Beechwoods have often been referred to as cathedrals by the poetic and I understand why. The leaves even tasted nice when they were very new. Bluebells didn't seem to mind too much being picked and taken home and for a couple of days the sitting room was filled with their perfume.

The Dip was a focal point of the village, as the area by the telephone box was the only piece of flat land in the village and therefore the only place where the annual fete could be held. A public holiday was held on the last Monday of May. It was tied to the Christian calendar and the celebration of Pentecost and called Whitsunday and therefore the holiday was called Whit Monday.

Anxious eyes were kept on the weather as fete day approached. My dad was enlisted to use the tractor to mow the grass a few days before the fete. Using the edge of the wood as protection from the sun, wooden trestle tables were set up for things like jumble (second-hand clothes), cakes, preserves and something called the white elephant stall, which was odds and ends of glass, china and silverware. You could purchase cups of tea and slices of cake or scones with jam and cream. There were competitions for the Best Ankles! There was a chocolate wheel. This name mystified me but you bought a ticket with a number on, the wheel was spun and a prize was given if the wheel stopped and the pointer was on your number.

The fete was organised by the local Women's Institute as a fund raiser. There was strong competition among the ladies for prizes in the cake-making and preserves categories. The genteel ladies sometimes had to be carefully reminded that they were ladies. But the competition was just as fierce among the men when vegetables were judged. I also remember men trying to catch a piglet!

At the end of the day when all this rivalry had finished, the tables packed away for another year, silence descended. Birds settled to sleep and the bluebells continued their gentle chiming as long shadows cast themselves over the land.

Dog Rose
Rosa canina

I grew up with the Flower Fairy books written and illustrated by Cicely Mary Barker. I have my favourites and one of them in *Flower Fairies of the Summer* is the Wild Rose Fairy. I find there is something particularly appealing about her. The wild rose is also known as the dog rose, hedge rose and briar rose. I once read that all roses have grown from this one and came to Europe from the east, a bit like tulips, which came from Persia. I don't know if that is true but I rather like the idea. It gives back some humility to all those hundreds of fancy varieties that seem to bring out the snob in people.

I remember English summer storms. The air would become so heavy and humid as enormous thunder clouds billowed and grew, inky hearts swelling by the minute. Suddenly a flash of lightning, a crack, crash and thunder rattled across the heavens and torrential rain would fall. We ran for shelter or be soaked to the skin in moments. We would count the seconds between lightning and thunder to know how far the storm was away, but when the windows were rattling, there was no doubt it was overhead. The storms didn't last long and, just as suddenly as they started, the rain stopped. The world paused as if to recover from the shock. Birds began to sing again. You could hear the water gurgling down the drainpipes and dripping off the guttering.

Country children learn early about storms. Electrical storms were beautiful to watch, lightning leaping like a wild creature among the clouds. I was frightened by the loud thunder but the real danger was in the forked lightning. We knew not to shelter under tall trees, as there was a strong possibility of the tree being struck. My dad had a tin lunch box and I can recall one afternoon he had to stop work because of the heavy rain and he was running along the path to the kitchen and forked lightning struck the ground near him. Was it drawn by the tin lunch box? I don't know. I do remember how shaken he looked when he came in and how concerned my mother was.

Riding Lane slopes quite steeply as it passes the Corner. After one of these violent storms, rainwater ran down the lane and gathered until it became a stream not a lane. It didn't take long to clear, as it eventually went down the drains about a mile away where the lane joined a proper road.

Mr Allan grew fabulous roses in his garden and after one of these brief storms I liked to go and look at them. They hung with bowed heads like ladies in crinoline dresses, though some still held their faces up waiting for the sun to dry the diamonds caught in their petticoats.

We only had two rose bushes in our garden. My grandfather planted them to grow over the old-fashioned wooden paling fence at the front of the farmhouse. Quite a lot of gardens in the village had pink or yellow rambling roses. Ours were miniature white ones. They had to be the most unfriendly flowers I have ever known, with their stems covered entirely by very sharp small prickles. But they were also pure magic. As buds, they were pale green and turned white as they opened to reveal a crown of yellow stamens in their centres. They had a wonderful perfume not like the larger roses at all. But it was hazardous to take a deep sniff, as they always had masses of green aphids all over them. They were horrible to try and cut to take indoors and so were left to ramble on the fence.

Lily-of-the-valley
Convallaria majalis

Nestled beneath the white roses my grandfather had planted lily-of-the-valley, a special favourite of my mother's. Whoever mowed the lawn had to take extra care not to cut down these shy flowers. (We also knew a hedgehog lived among the long grasses under the fence.) Although she loved their perfume, Mother rarely picked them to have indoors.

Having written that sentence, I need to explore that a little. I have a granddaughter who from a very young age always wanted to pick flowers. We could go for a walk and sure enough she would try and pick any bloom that took her fancy. She truly could see nothing wrong with this and no lecture about stealing made the slightest difference. And I'm not one to criticise at all, because I am exactly the same – and no, she didn't learn this from me, it came naturally.

All of my life, my fingers have reached out to pick flowers and I have had to make a conscious effort to stop. I am a flower child. Flowers will ever be my favourite people. They show such courage. Totally at the mercy of any passing creature who might trample or eat them or pick them. And at the mercy of the weather no matter what it does. Yet they have the capacity to come back from the brink time and time again. I want to pick flowers to become one.

Mother grew up in the town of Brighton on the south coast of England. By her eighteenth birthday, war was raging and she and her sister joined the Land Army in preference to working in a munitions factory. This was where she met my dad and at the end of the war they married and went to live at the farm. She always maintained that town people had a different and possibly better appreciation of the country because it was new to them. I am sure my love of flowers was influenced by her own love of nature.

As part of that harsh reality, our garden, while large, was used to grow vegetables. But we had a lilac tree by the garden gate to the farmyard which attracted many bees. Someone had beehives in the orchard a hundred yards or so from the garden and the bees were probably from there. They became really grumpy with anyone going through the gate.

Mother had a flower garden by the gate. I can recall deep blue delphiniums, vibrant orange marigolds, shy blue and pink forget-me-nots, snapdragons and old-fashioned pinks. There was another small garden patch for flowers by the back door. Mother grew goldenrod, miniature cornflowers (not the ones found in cornfields), lavender and peonies. This was where I grew my sweet peas. I liked best to buy a packet of seeds of assorted colours. That way, I didn't know till they actually bloomed what I had.

Sweet pea
Lathyrus odoratus

I loved the garden. I loved to help my dad when I was old enough to use a proper fork. He taught me how to push the prongs in to make a small clod, then to lift the earth and turn it over leaving a small trench the length of that patch. Next we put manure into the trench and dug the next row to cover it. Manure wasn't purchased from a garden centre. We kept pigs in the disused stables in the orchard and a pile of manure grew in close proximity. It was a wondrous sight to see the earth freshly turned and free of weeds that had grown over the winter.

There is an art to growing vegetables in straight lines and I confess it is an art I have never learned. No matter how hard I tried, my lines were alway crooked. And it wasn't because Dad didn't show me how. He measured the distance between rows with his footsteps. He had two sticks, one with string wound around it. He pushed one stick in at the end of the row and let the string unravel as he went to the other end and pushed the second stick in. Easy-peasy, as the saying goes: you have a straight piece of string held taut between two sticks. The problem arose when I had to use a dibber to make the hole to put the seed potato in or the runner bean, broad bean or pea seeds. I carefully made the holes, dropped the seeds in and just as carefully covered them up – like tucking the hyacinth bulbs into the ceramic log. But when the new shoots came up a few days later, it was clear my eye for a straight line didn't exist. Once the plants grew a bit, it didn't really notice too much but my dad was known to sigh at my ineptitude.

But there was more. Beans and peas needed sticks for support for the tiny tendrils they sent out. Dad would find slender sticks from the hazel hedges around the Top Meadows and also some with smaller twigs to help those baby plants get a good start. He never let me help him put the sticks in – easy to understand why. But he did give me the left over sticks for my sweet peas.

I used the same method of creating straight rows for my sweet peas, with the same results as the vegetables. I put my support twigs in and watched in wonder and delight as the plants flourished. They were rather all over the place but even Mr Allan, who grew his sweetpeas in perfectly straight rows with perfectly symmetrical bamboo canes for support, had to agree my sweet peas were often better than his.

Honeysuckle
Caprifoliaceae

The Country Diary of an Edwardian Lady by Edith Holden is one of my most treasured books. There are two distinct reasons for that. My mother sent me a copy many years ago and in it she, my dad and a couple of ladies in the village had written messages inside the cover. I hold it in my hands and am directly connected to people who knew me when I was a child. There are many advantages to being a migrant and creating a new life, but there is always the tug of those early years, with all the memories good and not so good.

The other reason is that Edith Holden did what I don't have enough skill or knowledge to do. Over the passage of a year, she wandered the countryside drawing and painting plants, butterflies, birds and small animals. She handwrote descriptions of what she had seen and added snippets of poems or country folklore quotes. I admire enormously her knowledge and her ability to share it in such a manner.

One of the difficulties with observations about nature is avoiding the repeated use of the word 'favourite'. I think of a particular plant or flower and for that moment it is my favourite. And so, when I look through Edith Holden's book, my eyes fall on the painting of dog roses and honeysuckle intertwined and I call it my favourite – because in this book it is. Why? In an instant, I am transported to the Top Meadows and the five-bar wooden gate that gave access through a dividing hedge. One side of the gate, forming part of the hedge, grew honeysuckle and on the other side serving the same purpose was a hedge rose. They both sent up long tendrils that wafted about in the breeze.

To get to the Top Meadows, I walked through the orchard of cherry, apple and pear trees adjoining the garden. It sloped upwards, so when I climbed through the hedge the world opened up. Why not go through the orchard gate? By following the hedge up the orchard, I came to the sheep pens and the sheep dip in the corner.

The sheep dip was a concreted deep narrow trench with steps at one end. The sheep were dipped before they were shorn to clean the wool and kill off any unwanted little livestock. Someone literally pushed the sheep in at the deep end. The trench being narrow, they couldn't turn and were guided with the help of a broom along the trench to the steps. They were also pushed under the water a couple of times to ensure that they were properly cleansed. They stumbled up the steps on to dry land and shook off most of the water. They were then guided through the gap in the hedge and out into the meadow beyond to dry and get on with what they did best – eat grass.

My love of wild flowers was nurtured as I wandered the meadows. Sadly, I don't remember the names now except for a few favourites. Ah, that word again. I did know which ones grew where. I could check out the honeysuckle and roses by the gate, find ground ivy in the hedgerows along with birds' nests, molehills and rabbit runs. If I went up there early in the morning, I could find field mushrooms as big as tea plates and bring them home. The secret was finding them before the sheep trampled on them!

On a warm afternoon, I could lie among the tall grasses, scabious, buttercups and clover trying to see the tiny black speck that was the skylark singing on high, music pouring down like sun-filled raindrops.

Foxgloves grew beside the hedge in the Top Meadows. How could

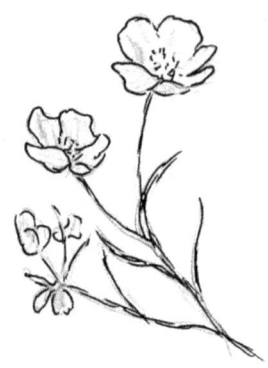

Buttercup
genus Ranunculus

Foxglove
Digitalis purpurea

I not call them a favourite? I wanted to put my fingers into their bell flowers but knew that, more likely than not, a bee would already be in there and they didn't like being disturbed. I've tried growing foxgloves here in my garden and they did look splendid briefly. There was conflict within, though. They needed lots of water, something I didn't even think about in England. We did have a covered well in the garden for watering the garden in a drought but I don't remember that happening very often. I just remember being told to never, ever stand on the old mossy rock that kept the lid on safely.

The sheep we had in the orchard and meadows were creatures of habit. Over the course of a day, they walked and ate their way around their territory – twice. Early in the morning, they would be close to our garden fence, by afternoon in the Top Meadows, then in the evening by the garden again.

After the sheep-dipping came the sheep shearing. The ultimate in fascination.

As I said earlier, we only had hot water for baths once a week. Every evening, though, my dad would stand at the kitchen sink to shave. He boiled the kettle and I was mesmerised as he used the pig-bristle brush to apply the special shaving soap. The best part was next. Watching him scrape the soap off his face. His razor was absolutely off limits, and I was not allowed to touch the blades – ever. How I worried if he cut his cheek! We had our rituals the same as the sheep, I suppose. The radio was turned on so that we listened to *The Archers* every evening as Dad shaved before he went to the pub for a drink.

Sheep shearing brought strangers to the farm. And it was with the same fascination of watching Dad shave that I watched the sheep being sheared of their fleece. How clean and small they looked without their thick grey-white fleece. I was fascinated how pale and creamy the fleece was close to the animals' skin. As soon as each sheep was released, they hopped, skipped and jumped to get away. It was lovely to watch how they were reunited with their lambs, who were noisily waiting outside the sheep pen for their mothers' return. How did they recognise each other in all that mass of bodies!

Lambing was another important time. Those poor little lambs born into cold and often snowy conditions! My dad used to go out at all times of day and night to check on sheep that were due to give birth. Sometimes, if a ewe had twins or triplets, it wasn't unusual for her to reject the smallest. Left alone, it would die. There were a couple of options. If another ewe had produced a dead lamb, a shepherd could take the skin off the dead lamb and wrap it around the rejected one. It was hoped the ewe would be tricked into believing it was her own lamb and accept it. If this didn't happen, then a rejected lamb would be hand-reared. It was here that Mary – from the Flower Pen – would step in. Every year she hand-reared a few orphans.

I remember one year Dad coming home late in the evening with an orphaned black lamb. We made a bed for it and fed it using an old-fashioned boat-shaped bottle with a rubber teat at each end and so kept it alive until morning when it would be taken to Mary's farm. A tiny lamb is surprisingly strong when hungry and it was hard to hold the lamb while stopping it knocking the bottle away. Milk seemed to go everywhere. Come morning, we couldn't find it. We could hear pathetic bleating and there it was hiding behind the black coal bucket in the kitchen. It was very well camouflaged.

Sheep can quite easily be moved from one paddock to another. They only need someone to lead them and they will follow. Moving a flock of perhaps a hundred sheep from one farm to another through a housing estate was challenging. The time chosen was early one Sunday morning so there was very little traffic. We had to keep them moving but not panic them into running.

The housing estate was typical of the area I grew up in, expensive houses and carefully manicured gardens; not all of them had fences. I've said I am no lover of roses but even I could see that many of the ones in these gardens were above average – enormous blooms, fantastic colours and highly scented. What a strange mix it was, a flock of noisy sheep being chivvied along the road so they didn't eat the lawns and flowers. The relief was palpable when we arrived at our destination, all sheep in and the gates securely closed. We also had the help of Lassie our sheepdog. She wasn't a family pet, she was a working dog and lived in an old barrel. A wire was tethered some distance into the orchard and her lead was threaded through it so she had room to run about when not working but still needed to be taken for a walk.

Gate closing was an important part of country living. With secure fences or hedges around them, sheep and cows seem quite content with their allocated meadow. Let one spot a gap in a hedge or a gate left open and they would concentrate their efforts to getting through to freedom. All very well, but these animals had no road sense – not that there were many cars about – or train sense.

City folks were the worst culprits going out to the country for the day. They parked their car somewhere and wandered through orchards and meadows without permission and too often left gates open. It wasn't unusual for Dad to be called out at any time because sheep or cows were on the road or train tracks. We were often taken along to help round them up and return them to safety.

Queen Anne's Lace
Anthriscus sylvestris

Queen Anne's Lace for me is another that makes up quintessential England. I knew it as cow parsley and it has several other names. As a little girl, it towered above me as I walked the lanes with Mother. It grew in great profusion by the barn next to the farmhouse close beside my bedroom and I used to pick it, peel the stems much like celery and eat them.

The barn was a simple single-storey wooden building with a low tiled roof and was almost as big as the house itself. I have gone to the internet to try and find what I'm looking for without much success. If the barn had been a boat, I could say it was clinker-built, with each plank horizontally overlapping the one below. It doesn't seem to be called that for a building. The closest I could find was something called shiplap walls. As it happens, Forty Green is about eighty miles from the sea, so not much chance of ship-building of any kind influencing the style of buildings – except that most barns in the area were built in such a way. Ours was painted possibly every year with creosote to keep it weatherproof. Time didn't matter much to a child, so I am guessing. I remember the smell of it, and the other lilac bush that grew close to my bedroom was often a temporary casualty of the painting.

The ground floor of the barn was lower than the yard outside. It had a dirt floor and four divisions where horses would have been kept in years gone by. Sometimes it was still called the stable. I mostly remember it as a place where sheep or pigs were kept when they were due to have their babies. The door was split in two so the bottom half was always bolted shut, but with the top half open, I could look in to see the new babies. At other times of the year, it was used to store bales of hay or straw.

The upper level was forbidden to me and probably my brothers too. It could only be accessed by the side furthest away from the house and you had to climb up a ladder, open the heavy door and step in. It was banned because the floor was unsafe. You could look between the wooden floor slats to the area below. I suspect now that wasn't the real reason. All kinds of old farming equipment was kept up there. Scythes and sickles were kept hanging from hooks from the ceiling beams and they were lethal, especially to a child. They were brought down in summer to cut the weeds from the embankment and along the narrow lanes. Except I didn't think they were weeds. Mother used to say weeds were just flowers growing on the wrong side of the fence. Cow parsley wasn't a weed, it just grew very tall and bushy and could make the narrow lanes very dangerous for cars. Our lanes were only single-track with sidings where a vehicle could go into allowing another to pass.

Joe Smith was an elderly man who was employed to cut down the cow parsley and stinging nettles. I loved to stand and watch him. We didn't talk. It was that mesmerising thing like Dad shaving and sheep being sheered. He taught me how to use both scythe and sickle but the scythes were too tall for me to manage safely and I could never quite get the knack of using the hooky stick to lay the plants down so I could slice them with the blade. I knew the theory but didn't have the skill.

These were the days before mechanical hedge trimmers that just slash everything to a uniform distance from the edge of the road. Hedging and ditching was an art form in those days – in fact, my brother Steve was still doing it recently in competitions. Again, I know the basic theory but have never actually done it. A hedge is made of living trees and bushes, mostly a mixture of different kinds like blackthorn, hawthorn, beech, hazel and so on. They need to be trimmed in winter or early spring. The idea is that you cut a tall stem but not all the way through. You then bend the stem and weave it through other vertical stems that have been trimmed shorter and to the height you want the base of the hedge to be. When new foliage grows, it creates an almost solid wall.

Hedges have formed boundaries between properties since forever and they also had a ditch on one side to allow drainage. The ditches had to be cleared of detritus so rainwater could run away. There is a complicated law about who owns which bit of property and the ditches were part of that, but as the child and now the adult, I don't think I need to know.

Herb Robert
Geranium robertianum

Hedges beside a lane or road were mostly growing on a small embankment and this is where the best wild flowers grew. I loved herb Robert. It was like a miniature cow parsley with celery-type stems, pretty lacy leaves and small pink flowers. Why such a favourite? Because of the smell. I wasn't a wise woman or herbalist in the making back then. I loved flowers because they looked pretty or smelled lovely. The value of their medicinal properties was lost on me.

Not so lost were wild strawberries that grew on the steep banks of the beechwoods. We had to travel about a mile and a half to primary school in Holtspur. It meant walking both ways to take my brothers to school and to bring them home. To save time, Mother would take her bicycle and, by her standing up to ride, I could sit on the seat. This worked quite well until, when I was about three or four, I was swinging my legs back and forth as she rode and my foot got caught in the spokes of the back wheel. I don't remember the fall that followed, just being anxious that to untangle my foot they had taken it out of my shoe and the shoe was left caught in the wheel. I hopped around on a cast as the greenstick fracture healed. I can remember when the cast was taken off and replaced with heavy elasticated bandage that stuck to my leg. This gave the needed support but it was hellish to get off. We had to soak it in warm water and try and peel it off a small section at a time. It hurt a lot.

But one of the advantages to these trips to and from Holtspur was watching the progress of the wild strawberries. We grew some strawberries in the garden but they required a lot of work. Straw was placed around the plants to keep the fruit from the earth and when fruit did appear we put empty jam jars on the ground and put the unripe fruit inside. The theory was that they ripened quicker but also kept the slugs and snails from eating them. Not entirely successful.

The wild strawberries had the same white flower but smaller. The tiny fruit glowed like a ruby and was smaller than a pea. But if you waited long enough for them to ripen properly, they tasted just as sweet as the garden variety.

Mrs Scarland lived in the village and had a son and daughter of similar ages to my older brothers. She was part of the walking home from school routine. She always seemed to be laughing. Mrs Scarland had copies of the *Winnie the Pooh* books by A.A. Milne and would loan them to us to read. I see Pooh has had yet another resurgence in popularity with Zen exchanges between him and Piglet. Such a hoot. But I remember the real thing. How blessed I was.

Mrs Scarland's daughter Judith was kind to a younger child. She gave me her doll's pram when she no longer played with it. It was my most prized possession. A replica of the English high pram, with big wheels, a storage space beneath the base and a waterproof apron to cover the baby. She also gave me a little blanket that she had made of dark green, pink and white woven squares. It also had a pillow and sheets with embroidered flowers on.

When I think about it, dolls were such a luxury item for my parents to buy and so they welcomed dolls given to me by neighbours. One Christmas, my parents made me a doll's cradle. Mother really didn't like sewing, though she could knit well enough. The cradle stood on four legs so it wasn't at ground level. The base was made of furniture webbing. An extra curved piece of wood was added to make a hood. That was Dad's work. Mother had cut up her summer frock of pink material to give the cradle a skirt and some net curtaining to use as an overlay and for the hood. It was this little girl's every dream come true. I could use the pillow and blanket from Judith's pram in the cradle as well. I had a baby doll with a pink lace dress that had been given to us. Another year, Dad made a proper doll's bed that sat on the floor. It was very basic but it came with a doll that if I tipped her over said, 'Mama.'

One morning, I woke to look down on the doll's bed to see a little mouse running across the pillow. My older brother came and rescued me.

Forty Green was situated in one of the wealthiest parts of England. Enormous houses with acres of grounds were the norm. Our closest town, Beaconsfield, was called a commuter town. It had grown around the railway station on the Princes Risbourough to London line, Hundreds of men took the train to London every day.

In our tied cottage on a farm labourer's wage, we had very little in the way of material wealth. There was an advantage living in the area, though – all our hand-me-down clothes and furniture were of good quality. Perhaps that's why as a child I didn't take any notice that we didn't have new things. I also give credit to Mother for this. She presented a new pile of clothes as a wonderful thing and I am certain it was for her as she tried to keep us all warm and clothed. She did a lot of knitting too – most of the village ladies did.

Auntie Alice was a champion in fine crochet work and won many prizes. As soon as she heard someone was having a baby, she created what was then called a layette. Tiny, delicate vests, matinee jackets, leggings, bootees, bonnets and mittens and a shawl were presented when the baby arrived.

Alice Bates was everyone's Auntie Alice. As a young girl, she also grew up in the old farmhouse I did. The house is hundreds of years old. At some time, her father bought a house opposite the pub and Alice looked after him there until he died. Alice was engaged to the man of her dreams but he was killed in World War I. She chose not to marry anyone else and so she lived alone for many years.

Set into the hedge at her house was the postbox. Many villagers would post their letters here rather than go into Beaconsfield. However, there was a price to pay. Auntie Alice sat in her bay window knitting and crocheting most of the time. Whenever someone came to the postbox, she would see them and call out to invite them in for a cup of tea and a biscuit. Impossible to refuse regardless of how busy you were. She had the most beautiful everlasting sweet pea plant by her front door.

I loved going into her front room. It was crowded with glass cabinets with heaven only knows how many miniature pieces of crockery, glassware and thimbles. I was allowed to look but I don't ever recall being allowed to touch anything.

Traveller's Joy or Old Man's Beard
Clematis vitalba

With the kiss of the sun for a pardon
The song of a bird for mirth
You are closer to God in the garden
Than anywhere else on earth

This was etched into a plaque in Mrs Curtin's garden. I loved it and it made perfect sense to me.

In the village was a wooden, single-storey, L-shaped building known as the WI hut. It had one main room with kitchen and toilet facilities to the side. The hut was used once a month for meetings of the Women's Institute and whist drives were held on Monday evenings and Wednesday afternoons. I used to go there for Sunday school on Sunday afternoons.

Forty Green had no church of its own. As part of Penn Parish, most villagers went to the Holy Trinity church in Penn, the next village. William Penn was a local man who lived from 1644 to 1718. He was a writer and a scholar and a member of the Religious Society of Friends (more commonly referred to as Quakers). He went to America and founded the province of Pennsylvania.

My parents didn't go to church except for Christmas, Easter or funerals. I had mixed feelings about the church even as a child. I didn't mind too much going to Sunday school; we did craftwork, making all sorts of things. I liked the smell of the glue, which came in a pot with a brush attached to the lid. The scripture lessons were stories that we were read and were interesting enough.

Going to church was different. Sunday morning for ten o'clock matins. I remember someone with a camper-van used to pick up various children in the area and take us to the church. I was fascinated by the van with its pull-down table, a stove and a sink and curtains on the windows.

The church was Norman, dated from about 1106 and made of flint. It was always bitterly cold inside. I liked the way the sun shone through the rich stained-glass windows, but I didn't like the dark nature of the figures. I always felt so very alone. Even on the occasions when Mother was with me, I felt lost. I couldn't follow the service in the missal. I never knew when I was supposed to be sitting, kneeling or standing. I liked the organ playing because there was an air of mystery. The organist was hidden behind heavy dark curtains and couldn't be seen, so it was as if the music thundered from nowhere. Even for the brief period my brothers Steve and Geoff were in the choir, I still felt small and alone.

Mr Muspratt the vicar gave a sermon from a high wooden pulpit and I was more interested in the wonderful inlay work it was made of, which formed engrossing patterns, than in whatever he had to say. The lessons were read from an enormous Bible that was placed on the open wings of an eagle that was the lectern. Again, the carved woodwork was fascinating. I never did know the significance of the eagle.

Many years later, I returned to look inside the church and spent time reading the panels on the walls. They were made of cement and etched into them were the names of local gentry in the past. The one that I smile over was a woman remembered for having twelve children and donating blankets to the poor. What a way to be remembered.

The pews at the front of the church had doors to them with brass hooks so, once in, it was tricky to get out. The pews were reserved for the gentry and I remember one day standing at the church door watching people going in, as I didn't want to go in alone. One kindly ladys insisted I go in with her and I sat in her special pew. I felt even more out of place than if I had been sitting in my usual place further to the back.

There was an elite boarding school for girls near the church and the girls would walk in pairs to the church and had specially allocated pews that no one else was allowed to sit in. I was intrigued by their uniforms and hats, because the primary school I attended had no set uniform.

The church bells were perhaps one of my favourite sounds from my childhood. I remember them ringing clearly across the fields and woods. We weren't allowed to go into that part of the church where the ropes hung down from the bells. Just once, I was taken up into the bell tower. It is said you could see seven different counties from up there. The church was set on the top of Beacon Hill. In the days before modern communication systems like radio, lighting a fire as a beacon from one high hill to the next was a very efficient way of getting important news across the country.

When I stepped out of the church, I felt I was freed from a heavy burden. I often walked home. It was downhill almost all of the way. Now was the time I could listen to birdsong and look for flowers in the hedgerows.

Opposite the church were the almshouses. These were tiny cottages built in a row for the poor, old and needy of the parish since the tenth century. Each had a small garden at the front for flowers and another in the back for growing vegetables. Apple trees are among my most vivid memories of those gardens.

Further down the lane lived a woman who my mother cleaned for once a week. Of all the things I can remember, it is the African violet in a large bowl at the foot of the stairs that is the keenest memory. How exotic it was. And when I went with Mother – probably in school holidays – I was given the task of preparing vegetables for the midday meal.

What made it special was the gadget for the runner beans. I had to cut the top and tails and the sides of each runner bean. Then I fed the bean through the gadget that cut them into narrow strips. And yes, I was guilty of eating quite a few.

The lane wound its way between high hedgerows till it came to Frying Pan Corner – a very sharp bend. Apart from being very dangerous for all road users and pedestrians, it was where the best old man's beard, or traveller's joy grew. Unlike the other wild flowers, it didn't seem to mind me picking it to take home. I was picking white fluffy seed heads on long strands that lay over the top of all the other bushes or up tree trunks. They didn't need water in the vase and they lasted for ages indoors.

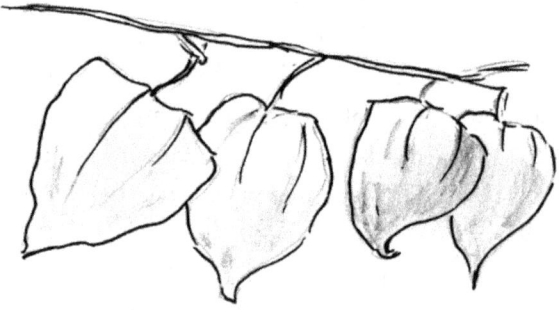

Honesty or Chinese lantern
Phylsalis alkekengi

In his garden, Mr Perfect had a plant called honesty or Chinese lantern. The flowers were brilliant orange and papery and didn't need water once picked. I was permitted to have some of them to go with the old man's beard.

Another unusual plant that grew along this lane was lords and ladies. It sent up a single stem covered in small round green berries. They were protected by thick green leaves that stood to attention. As autumn approached, the berries turned scarlet. They were poisonous too.

I always hurried past Longfield Wood, which climbed up from this part of the lane. Even after all these years, I can't explain the eerie feeling of being watched. If I was cycling, the speed I gained meant I could get all the way up the last hill. That brought me to Auntie Alice's house and one last swoosh downhill to the farmhouse.

Opposite Auntie Alice's house was the pub, the Royal Standard of England. I must be careful what I write now, because my childhood memories probably won't match the history to be found on the internet. As I learned it, Charles I or II hid in the pub while fleeing from England during the Civil War. He had the Royal Standard with him, but did he have it when he left? I remember being shown an enormous heavily embroidered flag or standard that was supposed to have been his. There was a connection between this and the pub being the only one in England entitled to call itself the Royal Standard of England.

In the summer, we used to walk up to the pub at Sunday lunchtime. Children weren't allowed inside, so we sat at the tables provided in the garden. By the front door stood an old penny-farthing bike. The publican would bring our glasses of lemonade and packets of crisps out on a tray and talked to us. The crisp packets had a small blue twisted paper bag which held the salt. It was very disappointing not to have salt to sprinkle over the crisps.

After dinner, or lunch as we would call it now, during spring, summer and autumn, we walked among the fruit trees. We were checking the progress of pretty blossom becoming tiny green cherries or apples. Then the ripening of fruit, whether it was being pecked by starlings and crows or damaged by rain. Today we see netting over cherry trees but it wasn't like that for us as children.

My dad hung bangers up in the trees. A piece of rope that smouldered slowly had firecrackers attached to it. It took about thirty minutes for the rope to burn from one firecracker to the next and the loud bang frightened off the birds, at least for a short while. The bangers were not popular among the neighbours as they did make a lot of noise.

One tree was a mystery. It had the prettiest, brightest, most succulent-looking cherries but they were inedible. They were grown specifically to be preserved and used as glacé cherries in cocktails and cakes, and to decorate ice cream.

Another Sunday afternoon ritual was being sent to Mrs Pusey to buy tomatoes from her greenhouse. She and her husband had a greengrocery in Old Beaconsfield. I was afraid of Mrs Pusey, as she always seemed so gruff. But hers was a hard life. Her youngest child was the same age as me and had Down's syndrome. He was very affectionate and very hard to understand. I was frightened of his tight hugs. Mother gave me a two-shilling piece and assured me I was expected. I was duly taken to the greenhouse – a miracle place for me – given a brown paper bag and told to fill it up. I could eat as many of the small ones as I wanted. Never in my life since have I tasted tomatoes like those. And I can still remember the smell of the broken stem on my fingers.

The neighbouring village of Knotty Green, about a mile or so away, had a cricket pitch equipped with a small pavilion. Throughout the summer, there were matches between other villages held here. After tea, we walked to watch the end of the game. It was a time where the adults could catch up with news and meet friends they did not see during the week. Children could play once the cricket match was over. Once, my uncle called to my brother to keep his eye on the ball. He took it too literally and the ball hit him right in the eye. He had a dreadful black eye and I can still recall the smell of witch hazel which his eye was bathed in.

The pub, the Red Lion, opened for trade at seven o'clock and as children we sat outside to drink our cherryade and watch cars go by. I am talking about the 1950s and there were few cars on our country lanes. We used to collect their numbers.

Walking home in the twilight was hazardous, as midges and gnats came out and left unpleasant bites on exposed skin. The air was also filled with the smell of newly cut grass.

White Daisy
Bellis perennis

We were blessed with a large garden which was mostly used to grow vegetables. There were two small areas of lawn in front of the house, divided by a path from front door to the garden gate.

I quite liked using the lawnmower, not a fancy one with an engine– ours had to be pushed along and had a catcher for the cut grass which was unloaded onto the compost heap. But like most things there was a downside – at least as far as I was concerned. Sunday was lawnmowing day. Our lawns were a mass of tiny white daisies and I often ran out there early to pick the daisies before Dad came along and mowed them down. Why picking them was less barbaric I have no idea. I hated to see the daisies damaged among the grass cuttings yet at the same time I liked the look of the lawn where it was clean and bright green. It was the same thing as watching Dad shave and sheep being sheared. The lawns had the added advantage of being mown with patterns. The cut grass was different depending on which way the mower was pushed. I'm not sure Dad really had the time for such finesse – it was just another job to be done in the hours when he wasn't working on the farm – but he did give in to my requests for a stripy lawn.

We grew mint in one area that had planks of wood to form a border around it. Mint doesn't understand the principles of borders. It sends out long runners as far as it can, which in our garden meant into the lawn. The smell of newly mown mint is as luscious as the smell of new-mown grass.

I liked making mint sauce. Mother had a small chopping board and a small vegetable knife. There was quite a knack to picking the mint, washing it under the tap to remove livestock like caterpillars, then plucking the leaves from the stems and starting to chop. Having a sharp knife was a bonus, and I held the knife at the pointed sharp end of the blade and moved the handle up and down in a chopping action. It sounds easy, I know, but it was also easy to slip and send bits of mint leaf flying across the table or onto the floor. When it was finely chopped, it was put into a small jug, a teaspoon of sugar added and just enough hot water to melt the sugar, before the vinegar was poured on. There was nothing quite like it on roast lamb! If I had my way, I would have had mint sauce on every dinner.

We had a mincer for leftover roast meat which Mother made into a shepherd's pie or cottage pie for dinner the next day. The mincer was made of heavy iron and was clamped onto the edge of the kitchen table. If it wasn't secured properly, it made the whole task much harder. The meat was cut into cubes about an inch square and fed into the mouth at the top. The handle was turned and this turned the screw piece at the base around. This screwing acting dragged the meat in and pushed it along to come out through a round plate with holes in. It would also drag in unwary fingers if you let them get too close.

When all the meat was minced, we put through a slice of dry bread to make sure it was cleared of meat. No waste! All this had to be dismantled and washed and dried carefully and put away until the next week.

Knives in our kitchen were a source of tension, I seem to recall. It was all about keeping them sharp. Too sharp made them dangerous for us children but I remember Mother's frustration slicing bread with a blunt blade and at some point being given the luxury of a serrated-edge bread knife.

In post-war England, there was no sliced bread for us. I can remember Mr Bristow the baker. He had his bakery in Old Beaconsfield but he delivered loaves to our village on Tuesday, Thursday and Saturday evenings. What I didn't know then was that he probably shouldn't have been driving at all as he did like an alcoholic beverage. Freshly baked bread has its own distinctive smell and while I didn't particularly like the crust when eating a sandwich, I did like the very end of the bread, some call it the heel. Cut thinly and spread with butter and sprinkled with salt – mmm. It was a sad day when Mr Bristow stopped delivering bread and sliced loaves were available from the supermarket.

I remember the days before the supermarket came to town. Mr Moffet delivered a cardboard box of groceries one day during the week. In it was sugar in dark blue paper packets, tea leaves in green paper packets, flour, orange concentrate and cod liver oil. Rationing finally came to an end in 1954. I hated the orange concentrate as it was so bitter but quite happy to trade my orange juice for my brothers' share of the cod liver oil.

Milk was also delivered every day. In summer, it had to be brought in quickly and the glass bottles stood on the cold flagstones of the pantry floor. No fridge for us then. Winter was far more interesting. The milk bottles were left by the back door and when it was deeply cold the cream would lift the foil lid up about an inch. It looked comical, but more than that, the blue tits and robins liked to come in and peck at the frozen cream. How pretty it looked but good old practicality came to the fore and the milk was brought in as quickly as possible after delivery.

But going back to sharp knives. We always had a roast dinner on Sundays, served at lunchtime. It was Dad's task to sharpen the carving knife, I loved to watch the criss-cross action of knife blade against the steel. He did try to teach me – was it hold the steel steady and pass the blade over it or the other way round? I didn't get it right then, so small wonder I don't remember. I had a tendency to blunt the blade even more! I do remember the lessons on how to carve a joint of meat, cutting across the grain just like when we sawed wood, and with a leg of lamb the blade going down to connect with the bone.

As I said, our garden was used to grow vegetables and Sunday morning had its own ritual. Potatoes had to be dug. There was an art to placing the fork far enough from the base of the potato plant to limit the number of potatoes that were stabbed by the tines. Then the magic of loosening the soil and lifting it all up to discover the potatoes beneath. I loved best the very small ones at the beginning of the season, boiled in minted water and served with knobs of butter on them. But necessity meant they had to be left in the ground to grow much bigger. All through summer, my dad would dig potatoes in the evening, just enough for the next day's dinner. I can still hear the clink of the fork tine against a stone left in the ground.

I helped pick peas, runner beans, broad beans, carrots and cabbage then sat on the back doorstep to prepare them for cooking.

Potatoes and carrots only need scrubbing to get their skins clean. Shucking peas was sometimes hazardous, as tiny caterpillars like to feed off the small peas and had to be removed with minimal waste. And yes, I ate far more raw ones than I should have. I did wish so many times we had the runner bean gadget I described earlier, but I had to make do with the vegetable knife.

The radio was on a lot on Sundays. There was a church service, possibly recorded from different churches throughout England and at noon came *Two-Way Family Favourites*. It was a request programme, so there were all kinds of music played for the British Armed Forces stationed overseas, connecting them with their families in England. I remember mystery names like Cologne, Aden, Cyprus and Butterworth.

My dad used to go to the pub when *Family Favourites* came on and we had to wait till he came home at about one to have dinner. We had a large round table with a central leg in the sitting room. It was made of walnut and very heavy. It was one of the few things Mother took with her when she eventually had to leave the farmhouse and she still had it when she died in 2019 a few weeks before her ninety-fifth birthday.

One Sunday, relatives arrived and we had eleven people seated round the table. On this occasion, Mother had her dinner in the kitchen, pleading the lack of space, but in fact she was eating her meal from a baking dish, as there weren't enough plates.

Newspapers were delivered every day too. Both of my older brothers did paper rounds to earn enough money to buy new bicycles and they had to do this before going to school. The papers were sorted at the newsagent in Beaconsfield and delivered to the telephone box in the village. They had two rounds. The short one was just the village and I often used to help at weekends. It was difficult sometimes to fold the papers up to post them through the letter boxes in front doors. If the bundle was too tight, the papers were torn when removed by the householder and complaints were made. The longer round was to the big houses on the main Beaconsfield to Penn Road. Each house had a very long drive. I went once with Steve but I didn't ever deliver papers for him.

The rewards were had by my brothers. Steve bought a red bike that had drop handlebars – very grown-up. Geoff's bicycle was green and, for reasons even he cannot remember, was called Tinkerbell. I only ever had plain black bicycles – second-hand of course – but somehow I didn't mind, because it was better than walking. To this day, I still prefer to ride my bicycle than to walk.

A lot of the village ladies cycled in those days. Mrs Fletcher had a wooden box attached to her bicycle just behind the saddle so she could put her groceries in it. String bags were used a lot too; they were hung from handlebars and made cycling quite precarious, but we had no bus service and few people had cars.

Fuchsia
Fuchsia circaea

Every summer during the school holidays, we went to visit my mother's sister, who lived close to the sea at Brighton. If you look at a map of the British Isles, you can see that Forty Green was about as far away from the sea as you could get. My parents had to decide whether we would go before or after the crops were ready to be harvested. I have no idea how such decisions were made.

The whole journey would take about four hours from door to door. Two large suitcases appeared and clothes enough for a week packed away. My dad carried those suitcases a mile or so to the railway station. The next part of the journey was a steam train that carried us to Marylebone Station in London and took about three-quarters of an hour. The railway lines ran past the Top Meadows and I liked to watch the smoke forming patterns like clouds as the train sped along.

My brothers, with Terry and Alan from the village and I, sometimes went to the chalk pit. Hogback Wood ran along the far side of the Dip and ended where the railway line was. The chalk pit was a large hollow – presumably created when chalk was taken. It had steep sides which we ran down. Part of the sense of danger was how close we were to the trains that passed on their way to Beaconsfield Station.

Another thing about trains I liked was where the road went over the railway line at Beaconsfield High Street. When the trains went underneath, we could be enveloped in the billowing smoke with its distinctive smell. And there was the mystery of the tracks dividing on the approach to the station. The usual two tracks became four and express trains and goods trains would trundle through on the central two while the passenger trains paused at the station.

The ticket office was the first place we went. Return tickets were bought. I listened carefully but really didn't understand how the ticket officer knew we were going to Brighton and then coming home again. We had to stand well back from the platform edge because of the steam. We bundled into the carriage, which had bench seats on either side covered in prickly velvety material which was horrid on bare legs. Dad heaved the suitcases up onto the luggage racks and we were off on holiday. Of course we wanted to open the windows and look out, but that was fraught with danger from flying cinders. They hurt so much when we got them in our eyes.

Houses and gardens seen from a railway carriage are so revealing. A window into another world. The approach to London was lined by endless industrial buildings, so bleak and faceless. The train had to go slower and seemed to take ages to pull into the station.

Excitement of a different kind now. We had to get to Victoria Station on the other side of London and to do so we went down into the Underground railway system. The escalators seemed to go down forever and we had to be sure we stood to the side so people in a hurry could go dashing past. Fancy walking on a moving staircase. The white-tiled walls were covered in advertising boards but I have no memory of what was on them.

I didn't like the Underground much. So many people, all in a rush. No doubt a family such as ours was a hindrance. There are different lines in the Underground that were at different levels going on different routes. I only remember two names, the Circle line and the Bakerloo line. We went on one line to Charing Cross then had to get off that train and walk along more tunnels, up or down stairs, to the next line that took us to Victoria Station. The lines were and still are all colour coordinated. The trains whooshed in and we had to jump on quickly before the doors closed. Then off we went into the tunnel and the walls were so close to the train. I liked looking at the map up near the ceiling. We could keep check of the names of the stations as we passed through them. They showed as straight lines on the map, but they curved in reality.

At Victoria, we had to go up the steep escalator to come out into the bright light of day. How strange it felt after being in the tunnels for probably three-quarters of an hour. I felt much happier out in the open. There were large destination boards that had to be studied to see when the next train to Brighton was; they had wooden slats that turned to hide the print when a train had just left. These were electric trains, vastly different to the steam ones.

We could get the Brighton Belle express train, which took an hour and didn't stop at all along the way. My grandad used to drive the Brighton Belle but I didn't ever see him in the engine. We were actually going to Preston Park, which was the stop before Brighton, so we caught the slower train. I don't remember how long it took. I do remember that the carriages had corridors so you could walk about.

There is a series of long tunnels on the London–Brighton line. Somewhere on the far side of them in the South Downs were the Jack and Jill windmills or the Clayton Windmills. I loved to look out for them, as they were all part of the wonder of our holidays.

Eventually, the train stopped at Preston Park and we had to walk to Grandad's house, where my aunt lived with her son. She was widowed less than two years after she married when the war ended.

Walking to Herbert Road was strange. Down and up hilly streets to a main road where the trolleybuses used to run into Brighton. The main road had a wide stretch of grass down the centre with huge horse chestnut trees.

Herbert Road was a steep hill lined with terraced houses. The house had only a walled-in tiny garden with a fancy mosaic path to the front door. There was a large fuchsia bush and I was entranced by the ballerina flowers, but it was also the easiest way for me to recognise my aunt's house from all the others that looked the same. There was also a plant called London pride (*saxifraga xurbium*) which I hadn't ever seen before. Number 3 had a back garden too but nothing like we had at home. Outside the back door was a tiny courtyard area where the outside toilet and the coal shed were, then up a short flight of stone steps and stepping into the small garden that was oblong-shaped with gravelled paths in the shape of the capital letter E. Straight lines in a garden, my goodness.

The real attraction of course was going to the beach. We caught one of the trolleybuses at the end of the road and always hastened to sit in the front seat upstairs for the best view. There were wonders to spot year after year – the Royal Pavilion with its white onion domes and minarets, the Old Steine where the buses terminated, and a large fountain which was lit up by alternating rainbow-coloured lights. Pure fairyland for this child. Close by was the actual beach and Palace Pier.

Palace Pier was a source of terror and delight. I didn't like the small gaps between the slats of wood that made up its surface. If I looked, I could see the sea, which was constantly moving and mostly dark green/grey. The English Channel is known for its rough currents and I make no apology for being afraid of the enormous waves that came crashing to shore. On the other hand, on the pier I could ride on the helter-skelter and watch my brothers and cousin go on the bumper cars.

The beach was not my favourite place either. Starting from the pathway, the stones were as large as a child's fist and smooth – sort of easy to walk on. This gave way to shale, which is much smaller pieces and sharp and horrible to walk on in bare feet. This eventually gave way to sand, which in my innocence I cried over because it was like mud. Paddling was fraught with danger because the waves seemed so big and strong and wanted to drag me back out with them. Hmm – not a water child then.

My parents used to hire a couple of deckchairs, which they set up on the shale, and us children were encouraged to build sandcastles and decorate them with shells and feathers. The chairs were tricky to erect and pinched severely unsuspecting little fingers. My dad used to roll up his trousers to his knees, tie four knots in the corners of a clean handkerchief to make a hat and go paddling. He derived such pleasure from it. I was surprised he had such white legs; at home I only ever saw his weatherbeaten face, neck and forearms, where he rolled his sleeves up for most of the year.

At some point, we wandered along by the small shops close to the beach, where we could have soft-serve ice cream – not available from the Walls ice cream man at home. A special treat for Mother was to have a chocolate flake in hers. Also we could have toffee apples or candyfloss – things usually only available at Beaconsfield Fair.

We walked among the twisting narrow Lanes with fun shops with antiques and all sorts of things. Stories of smugglers filled the air but I found the crowds frightening and was careful not to lose sight of my parents or brothers.

We took a ride on the double-decker buses that had no roof out to Black Rock with its huge white cliffs. We clambered over a large area of dark rocks and hidden pools and collected winkles.

Mother became a different person on holidays. For all her learned appreciation of the country, she was a town girl before the war and loved to look around the large department stores. My aunt was still a town woman with smart clothes and careful make-up and the sisters were quite different.

Each year, one of us children was left to stay with our aunt for another week and she would then bring us home and stay with us for a week. When it was my turn, she treated me like a girl. She took me shopping for frilly underwear and to see her friend, who had a knitting wool shop in the basement of her house. Such colours! And there was Great Auntie Min. She was very genteel, again very town smart, and always smelled lovely and gave me scented soap to take home. When I say she treated me like a girl, I mean no criticism of my parents. I had two older brothers and tagged along wherever they went. I was treated just the same as them when it came to climbing trees and sawing wood, and I had learned it was a way of getting attention to be like the boys.

Poppy
Papaver rhoeas

Home again from our holiday at the seaside and the joy of reacquainting myself with familiar haunts. Going in the front door always felt odd. That might sound strange but the front door was always left locked and the key left in the lock on the inside. Part of my dad's routine was last thing at night to bolt the back door.

We may only have been away for a week or so but the garden in that time had run wild. So many peas, runner beans and broad-beans to be picked. Check to see if the birds had eaten all the raspberries or were there enough for tea. The lawns a wonderful array of long grasses bedecked with clover, buttercups and daisies. Mother used to say we had meadow grass, not a lawn.

Checking the chickens. A neighbour would have been asked to collect the eggs each day but it was usually one of my jobs. The chicken house was a wooden shed on two wheels and this made it easy to move

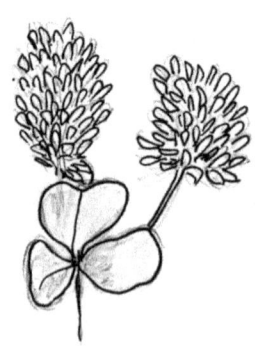

Clover
Trifolium pratense

around the penned-off area. I wasn't very keen on putting my hand under a sitting hen to see if she had eggs there but I did like searching in the pen among the weeds and underneath their house to see if there were stray ones not laid in the proper nesting boxes. The hens were encouraged to do this by white china eggs left in the nesting boxes. It was only a real issue if the hen was getting broody, as they could give a vicious peck if they didn't want to part with her future babies.

One year, I found a different use for the china eggs and had nothing to do with encouraging the chickens to lay eggs. April Fool's Day was an important day in our calendar. We could play jokes on each other with no fear of retribution when the triumphant call went up, 'April Fool.' Once, I remember putting a china egg in an egg cup and served it to Geoff for his breakfast. I must have been feeling creative that year because Steve was often heard to say he was so hungry he could eat a horse, so I took one of our toy horses – Clumpy the carthorse, to be precise – and placed it between two slices of bread for his breakfast. I'm not sure either of my brothers appreciated the joke. All jokes had to end by noon. If you tried playing a joke after that, the victim had every right to pay you back in some way.

Like most children, I expect, memories of school summer holidays were that they seemed endless. My brothers have some tales to tell about harvest time that I was excluded from because I was a girl. Living on a farm was potentially dangerous. Back then, there were few safety laws.

In early spring, the fields beyond the orchards were ploughed in preparation for wheat, oats or barley. They were then harrowed, which broke down the soil. The next part of the process was when the drill came along. It was designed to make a groove in the soil and put seed corn and fertiliser into the groove. The field was harrowed again to cover the seeds. Before being taken out into the field, the drill had to be properly checked. I liked to help to this. The drill was about six feet wide, with two long boxes each divided in half. One box held seed, the other fertiliser. From those boxes were tubes that reached down to the ground and each had its own little lid so you could govern how much seed was planted. These tubes had to be kept clear and allow the seed and fertiliser to run free. When the corn grew in its orderly lines, you could always tell where the drill tubes had become clogged and no seed planted.

A field of growing corn has its own magic. While still rich emerald green, the wind blowing through it made it move as if a giant hand was brushing it in patterns. Gradually, with the hot sun, it ripened and anxious eyes were kept on those summer storms. One heavy shower could flatten the stems and much of a crop would be lost forever. A field of corn is never just that. Among the growing gold were the red poppies – brilliant splashes of colour – so beautiful but not welcomed. For me, one of the sad but precious things about the scarlet poppies was their fragility. The stems were strong but the petals were tissue-thin and even the lightest touch bruised them and caused them to crumple. Much hardier were the vivid blue cornflowers and white ox-eye or moon daisies. How I loved all these flowers. Why on earth were they called weeds and considered a nuisance among the corn? I may be a farmer's daughter but I am ever a flower child at heart and the conflict within is very real at times. I don't like having to be sensible and logical about some things.

Ox-eye daisy
Leucanthemum vulgare

Often, at the very outer edge of the corn stems, grew scarlet pimpernel and the delicate blue speedwell. Pimpernels stayed open in the sun, but as soon as a cloud came over they closed up – just like the celandines. Some people used them to read the weather by, but clouds don't necessarily mean rain, do they? Speedwell flowers were like little cups of blue sky down on the earth. Both these flowers grew very low, with stems too short to make much of a posy.

Harvest time was dangerous for everyone, men and animals alike. The combine harvester seemed huge. The large blades at the front cut the corn and pushed it back and the husks were thrashed from the stems. The corn poured out into waiting sacks and the chaff fell out behind the harvester. Someone had to stand on the platform and, as the sacks filled, they had to be pulled away and an empty one put in its place. While the next sack was filling, the full one had to be stitched closed.

A tractor followed the combine harvester with a baler. This picked up the chaff and packed it tight into straw bales held together with twine. These had to be collected as soon as possible so they didn't get soaked in one of those summer showers.

The combine harvester needed two men to operate efficiently. One to drive, the second taking care of the sacks of corn. One of the men had a rifle to hand. Again, that hard practical side to farming. The standing corn had become a home for rabbits, and foxes liked the rabbits. When cutting the corn, you start at the outside and work round and round the field towards the middle. This means that animals hiding would keep moving ever closer to the middle but at some stage they would have to make a mad dash for freedom and life and try and get to the cover of the hedgerows. The rifle was used to shoot as many of the rabbits and foxes as possible.

One year, there was a tragic harvest. A man from a neighbouring farm came to help and, against all his knowledge of a lifetime working on a farm, he left his shotgun leaning against the ladder of the combine. He had climbed down to have a break and a welcome drink of cold tea. Climbing back up the ladder, he jogged the gun, and because he had not put the safety catch on, it discharged its deadly load into him. It was a terrible day for everyone, bringing home in a brutal fashion so many of the laws of country life.

There is more to harvest time that making hay and cutting corn. The three orchards behind the farmhouse were filled with fruit ready to be picked. Cherries were first to ripen. Some time before they were ripe, the ladders were taken out of the stables where they lived resting on the overhead beams. Each ladder had to be checked to ensure that the rungs were all sound. Any needing repairs were loaded onto the lorry and driven to Hazelmere, about six or seven miles away. I loved these short trips when I was allowed to go with my dad. Nothing special happened except I had him to myself for a while. I don't think we talked much, though I was often referred to as a chatterbox, but I have no idea what we might have talked about.

We children were allowed to climb up the ladders to help pick cherries. We had a round wooden basket each with a piece of rope looped through the handle. A large hook was attached to the rope and was either slung off the ladder rungs or from a branch while the picker filled the basket. Climbing down was difficult because the basket was heavy, and the fruit was then poured into waiting half-bushel or bushel wooden boxes.

Mother was always given a basket of cherries that she preserved. This is where the pantry came into its own. By the end of harvest time, the shelves would be filled with bottles of cherries, blackberry and apple and pears, which went a long way to feeding her hungry family during the winter.

Itinerant workers came to the farm for a few days to help pick the cherries, which had to be picked quickly before the birds ate them, or rain damaged them, and taken to Brentford market. To assist in this, didikois were employed for a few days. A didikoi is the offspring of a Romani gypsy and a non-Romani. The laws for the Romani gypsy are strict and folks with mixed blood were outcasts. The ones that came to the farm were a family of travellers moving from workplace to workplace. I can still hear a girl a bit older than me calling me from the orchard, 'Eh you...' She just wanted someone to play with. I was puzzled and asked Mother why she called me A-you as if it were my name.

One summer, my dad let me go with him to the market. It meant getting up very early. I don't remember anything but the noise and raised voices, and on the way home we called in to see my grandparents, who lived in Great Missenden.

My dad was a heavy smoker and rolled his own cigarettes. That was not possible when driving the lorry to market and I learned how to make the cigarettes with the roller the night before. It was supposed to produce even cigarettes but it was much harder to do than you would think. He was very patient with my efforts.

Apples and pears didn't have the same urgency to be picked. I had a swing hanging from a branch in the apple tree in the garden. I spent countless hours under this leafy canopy, trying to get high enough to touch the branches overhead. The apples were the beautiful green ones that Mother used for apple pies and for preserving. We had to pick blackberries to go with them. Blackberries grew in the hedgerows and had dreadful prickles the length of their long canes. The fruit had to be just ripe – too red and hard, they were inedible; too soft, they often had maggots in them. But they were delicious and of course we ate as many as we put in the bucket to take home to Mother. Folklore says blackberries shouldn't be picked after 10 October because the devil has spat on them. The devil was supposed to have fallen from heaven on 11 October, landed on a blackberry and spat on it, thus making it watery and not so good to eat. Of course in reality they were older by then and not so good for preserving but folklore was used to teach us important lessons.

The big pear tree in the orchard had the most beautiful blossom but the brown pears never seemed to ripen. I'm sure they did, but pinching one off the bough was never very rewarding.

At the end of summer, all the potatoes had to be dug up. They were laid on hessian sacks to dry properly in the sun and all dirt brushed off. They were also checked carefully for slugs. They were then put in half-bushel boxes and stored in the dry darkness of the pantry. It was hoped there would be enough to last all winter and ones only had to be bought from the greengrocers if we ran out before the new potatoes were ready the following year.

Our chickens were very obliging with eggs most of the year but never as many during the cold winter months. To this day, I shudder at preserved eggs. Not the taste – Mother only used them in cakes – but the stuff they were preserved in. Water-glass. We called it egg-glass but whatever its name, it was a solution made of sodium silicate. Mother filled a tin bucket with this stuff and eggs were carefully put in and a cover of some kind put on. It was often my job to get eggs out of the bucket for use. The water-glass was white, thick, slimy and very cold. Yuk.

A much nicer stone storage jar was used for pickled onions. We had a salad patch where Dad grew beetroot, radishes, lettuce, spring onions and shallots. Shallots were pulled from the ground before they grew too big; the skin was taken off and they were placed into the stone jar in malt vinegar. A lid of brown paper tied on with string finished the job and then we had to wait a few weeks before they were ready to eat.

Boiling beetroot: now that I do remember. Like potatoes, the small ones tasted the best; once they grew larger they went woody. Mother did preserve some in vinegar, but mostly they were eaten with a dollop of Heinz salad cream. No fancy mayonnaise for us, it was always salad cream and I still enjoy it. Radishes were fun. We cut the tops and tails off and cut a star shape at one end and put them in a glass of cold water. Very quickly, they opened up like flowers.

Rhubarb was popular. When it first started sending up new shoots, an old tin bucket with holes in the bottom was placed over the plant so the stems grew tall reaching for the light. Lessons learned all those years ago have stayed: you pull the ripe stem from the crown of the plant but never eat the white part below the pink stem as it is poisonous.

Jam making was another thing that had to be done. Raspberry jam is the best when you have picked the fruit, made sure the centre core has been pulled out and then the fruit weighed. It was an equal amount of fruit to sugar. A dangerous task, though, when stirring the bubbling jam. Testing it for readiness, that required a small amount put onto the back of a metal spoon. If it formed a sort of skin, then it was ready. Jam jars were kept year after year. Once poured into the jars, a circle of greaseproof paper was placed on top of the jam, and then a larger circle of clear cellophane was put over the top of the jar and held in place by an elastic band.

There was a special treat for Mother – perhaps because she seemed to be the only one who really enjoyed it. Apricot jam. She bought a pound of apricots – a luxury item – and made them into jam. They had a stone in the middle that had to be cut out and the kernel was put into the jam. I do remember being told never to eat the kernels raw as I would any other nut because they were poisonous. Perhaps there was something in the boiling that made them safe to eat.

Calendula
Calendula officinallis

Forty Green sits just over a mile from the nearest village or town in any direction. A mile or so to go to primary school in Holtspur, a mile or so to go to church in Penn and a mile or so to go to Beaconsfield for doctors, shopping and the library. With no bus service to the village, it was walking or cycling for most people when they went anywhere.

Grocery shopping in Beaconsfield was a real issue for some of the elderly in the village and my mother stepped in to help whenever she could.

Mr and Mrs Perfect lived across the lane in an old flint cottage with only a cold water tap in the kitchen, a chemical toilet down the garden and no gas or electricity. They used the old-style paraffin lamps for lighting and a wood-burning range to cook. Mrs Perfect always had the kettle on the boil. Mother called in every day to see if they needed any help, as Mr Perfect was stone-deaf and Mrs Perfect was crippled with arthritis. Their floors were old flagstones and very uneven with so many years of people walking on them, which made it very difficult for Mrs Perfect with her walking stick.

Mother always had to have a cup of tea when she visited. But she also did the shopping for them when she went into Beaconsfield to do her own shopping during the week. All carried home in bags hanging from the handlebars of her bicycle. Her reward was vegetables from their garden which their son grew. A kind of barter system.

Mother also called in on Mrs Jackson and Mrs Curtin – both with elderly husbands unable to go beyond the garden. Both couples had adult children to care for them but Mother's visits were something beyond doing a few bits of shopping. All kinds of news was shared and the basic thing of checking that they were simply safe and reasonably well and hadn't fallen.

Saturday morning was when Mother did our family shopping. I always went along to help carry things home. Oh, the mysteries of Sainsburys. The shop was divided in two – items needing refrigeration on one side and dry goods on the other. Butter was bought in whatever amount you needed and was cut off a large block and then two wooden paddles were used to pat it into an oblong shape. Cheese was sold the same way, and was cut to size. The large block of cheese was placed on a board with a narrow channel down the middle. A wire with a wooden handle was drawn over the block of cheese and, hey presto, a smaller piece to take home. Bacon and ham were placed on a different cutting machine and anchored to hold them still. The thickness of the slice was selected and, by turning a handle, the meat was sliced and fell neatly in a pile on the other side of the blade.

All of these processes held me mesmerised. We bought things like corned beef and luncheon meat, which were sliced to size and wrapped in greaseproof paper first then in white paper.

Next, we went to the other side and bought biscuits – not by the packet as we do now, but by the pound or less. Rich tea biscuits or, for a special treat, something whose name I don't recall. It was two round biscuits held together with jam, but the top biscuit had a hole in it so the jam poked through. But mostly we had a pound of broken biscuits. It didn't matter to us that they were broken; what was important was the different types in the bag and we all had our favourites.

Buying knitting wool was another beloved task. Mother knitted a lot for her family. I loved to look at patterns and choose the colour wool. She didn't have the money to buy enough for a garment in one go, and to ensure that the wool was the same dye lot, the lay-by system was invaluable. It was often knitting wool that she bought home for the ladies of the village who always had some garment being made.

Woolworths had a sweet counter and Mother bought treats to help us walk home with heavy shopping bags. The sweets were loose and sold by the ounce. Mother's choice was a quarter-pound of chocolate-covered peanuts, mine was a quarter-pound of chocolate-covered peanuts and raisins. Very occasionally, I had just two ounces of sugared almonds because they were far more expensive.

Then there was the newsagent. Papers were delivered as I have said and they were paid for on Saturdays. Mother used to collect my brothers' pay for delivering the papers.

The very last stop of all was the library. I wanted to be a librarian. I wanted to be able to work in that peaceful place, put books away, stamp the ones going out, being free to read whatever I wanted. How strict Mrs Brown was about anyone talking, even children. If a baby should start crying, the mother hastily left the building. Mrs Brown was kind too, making suggestions about what was or wasn't a suitable read for a young mind but endlessly encouraging.

The village may not have had most things expected but we did have a small shop at different times. Mr and Mrs Branham converted the front room of their house next to the pub into a shop. I can't remember what they sold other than sweets; no doubt it would have been general grocery items. Flying saucers were a halfpenny each and something fruity in pink paper cost a farthing each. I remember being introduced to a Biro pen. Mr Branham showed me how to make the ink flow in a new one by drawing waves on a piece of paper. For reasons unknown to me, the shop was only open for a short time and they left the village, but they came back to open another one.

Mr and Mrs Mellor lived opposite us. They had a wooden house at one end of their garden where they lived with their two daughters while a new brick house was built next to it. The new house was everything our house wasn't. Large. In fact, a large oblong box really. All the windows were the same – large. There was a glass door that opened from the lounge room onto a terrace, which seemed luxurious to me. But the best thing of all, the door from the front hall into the lounge room was also made of small glass windows and the doorknob was glass. I was fascinated by the design of the doorknob that seemed to catch the light and send out flashes of rainbows. They also had an antique clock in a glass dome and you could see all the inside workings of the clock.

Mrs Mellor and her sister had grown up in the Royal Standard of England pub and their parents were antique dealers. In the far-off days before the pub was sold and changed a lot, most of the downstairs rooms were used to store antiques, with just three small rooms used by the public.

When Mrs Mellor moved into their new home, this left the wooden house empty. The Branhams returned to the village to rent a house and part of the wooden house was converted into a shop. Again, the Branhams didn't stay long but the shop was taken over by someone unknown to everyone. A rather austere single woman – Miss Attwood – who never really became part of the village. My mother was employed to help at busy times and when Miss Attwood did deliveries or had to go to the wholesalers for provisions. The shop was patronised by the monied folks in the area and even I noticed that villagers would go in when Mother was there on her own. Like any village or corner shop, it was the hub where people could linger for a chat or gossip, which was something Miss Attwood didn't encourage.

Mrs Mellor seemed to hold herself separate from the villagers; her daughters were rarely allowed to play with me and, if that wasn't enough, they had a caravan which they took to France for holidays each summer!

The village had its fair share of characters. Mr Hine used to come to our house every weekday morning at about eight o'clock or sometimes after lunch. He had his own newspapers delivered but different ones to ours. I didn't know it then but he used to read our paper for the racing pages. He was a lonely and difficult man – a widower with a housekeeper. His only son had been shot down in the Battle of Britain and Mother believed he enjoyed the company of us children as he had none of his own. He owned a small orchard and the gate was at the Corner. For as long as I can remember, he had calves that leaned over the wooden five-bar gate. What was kept from me until I was older was that he fattened them up for market, sold them and bought more. In my innocence, I thought it was the same calves year after year.

There was an old railway carriage in the corner of his orchard – not one with passenger seats, rather an ordinary goods truck. There was a family who lived in it for years until a council house was available for them. I had strict instructions not to talk to them. I always had this sense of being sheltered and protected.

Hazelnut
Corylus avellana

Next to the railway carriage but separated by a tall hazel hedge lived Terry and his parents. They rented a simple house, two-up and two-down with a lean-to on part of the back where the kitchen was. There was no bathroom and they had a chemical toilet behind the kitchen. Terry's mother would come and have a bath at our house sometimes.

Terry spent a lot of time with us, playing endless games in Roundhead Wood. But I was sometimes invited to his house for tea. Such a treat to have beans on toast with a knob of butter on top – an unheard of thing. Terry's dad came from Beaconsfield but his mother was from London and so different to the other ladies in the village. She always wore smart clothes, high-heeled shoes, make-up and perfume. She worked for years in the post office, which was something else that set her apart – most young mothers were like my mother, home-based raising a family. They went to Lyme Regis every year for their summer holidays.

In post-war times, there were quite a few young families in the village. Mostly it was a villager who married someone from farther afield who then came to live in the village.

Sometime in the 1950s, a small estate of twenty-five council houses was built at the far end of the village. There was a lot of opposition to it and anyone living on the estate found it hard to integrate even though they might shop at the village shop, join the WI and go to the local pubs. Yet I can recall how pleased Terry and his parents were to be able to move into a brand-new council house in Holtspur. Opposite the primary school we went to were the old Nissen huts. As the families living in them were rehoused, the huts were demolished and new houses built.

The nearby towns of High Wycombe and Slough were where Mother went shopping, but not often. Most of our clothes were second-hand but there were times when she availed of the big department stores like Marks and Spencers for good quality but relatively cheap clothing, It entailed the mile or so walk to Holtspur to get a bus to either town and of course the return journey laden with bags.

The nearest hospital was in High Wycombe. I was taken there when I broke my ankle and again when I had my tonsils out. I recall it was winter and there was snow on the ground. I spent four days in hospital and because I was a tiny bit shorter than another child, I had to sleep in a cot not a bed. I was about four years old and not best pleased, because at home I not only had my own bed, I had my own bedroom. Sharing with other children in the ward was as frightening as not seeing my family at all. Everything was cold and bright. Oh, and the wretched toast we were given for breakfast the morning after the operation. I'm sure there was a good reason for it, but it certainly seemed harsh at the time. A neighbour came to collect me and take me home. Never had the dim sitting room with its log fire felt so welcoming.

Horse Chestnut
Aesculus hippocastanum

Autumn has always been my favourite time of year. Some say it was because I was born in autumn – on Hallowe'en or All Hallows Eve. There are many myths and legends surrounding 31 October (samhain) going back to the Celts of Ancient Britain and Ireland and perpetuated by the Romans with their own version. The date was considered the beginning of winter and the new year.

Where I grew up, folklore said the harvest had to be in by Michaelmas or 29 September. Hymns like 'We plough the fields and scatter…' and 'All is safely gathered in…' had special significance for us. Even my dad went to the Harvest Festival service.

For me, it was more about the dramatic changes that occurred all around. After the long light evenings of summer, suddenly the days grew shorter and I looked forward to getting home from school and sitting by the fire. I have written about sawing and chopping logs for the fire, but kindling was also needed. Mother was always busy but every day she would go for a walk in Roundhead Wood to gather small beech twigs to take home for lighting the fire. Or if we were playing in the woods or orchards, we were expected to bring home a handful of sticks.

Apple and cherry tree leaves turned yellow, orange, scarlet and crimson. Copper beeches did literally turn copper-coloured. I loved to walk in the woods and kick up the piles of dried and crunchy leaves. It was like walking through cornflakes. And the smell of damp leaves is unique. Emerald green moss grew in fat cushions and, covered in tiny brown stalks, each with a circle of minute tendrils, it looked like another miniature forest. Everywhere among the tree roots were small toadstools. There were many different kinds, even the red ones with white spots. One of the basic lessons for a country child is knowing not to touch or eat toadstools. No matter how pretty or appealing, some were deadly and better left alone. I remember the painstaking lessons about how to identify mushrooms by their smell and their beautiful pink pleated petticoats, but always, if in doubt, don't touch.

Autumn brought all kinds of surprises among the hedgerows. When the wild roses and hawthorn bushes were laden with brilliant red hips, it was a sign there would be a cold winter ahead. I was taught that nature had her own way of providing food for all. Rose hips were full of seeds, each one covered in tiny hairs that itched horribly. Children have some unpleasant traits and putting rose hip seeds or itching powder down someone's clothes so their back itched was one I remember all too well.

There were hazel hedges bordering the Top Meadows and some of the best nuts could be found there, but of course it was like getting to mushrooms before sheep trod on them – we had to get the nuts before the squirrels did but they were no good if picked while still green.

Beech mast or nuts were unusual as they were three-sided. They tasted good but they were hard to find among the fallen leaves. I think there must have been some very fat red squirrels in those beechwoods. Oak trees gave me acorns to make fairy tea cups out of. Oak trees and chestnut trees grow like giant umbrellas, good places to shelter from sun or rain for children and animals. Chestnut trees had the most amazing flowers, just like candles standing erect among the foliage. I have a fleeting memory of Dad bringing home a hessian sack of chestnuts. We

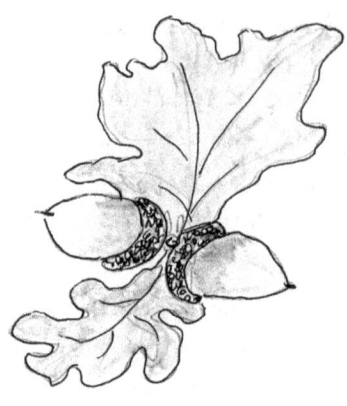

Acorn
genus Quercas

placed a few each evening in front of the fire to dry out to eat. I ate them raw, but Mother talked of eating them freshly roasted and served in a twist of newspaper like a cup. I still prefer mine raw.

Walnuts were a feast but oh so messy. I remember sitting on the floor in front of the fire shelling walnuts and how hard it was sometimes to get all of the kernel out. The real challenge was to get the kernel out intact. Our fingers were stained brown for days when we had been shelling walnuts – small chance of hiding the evidence if we tried to pinch any. Much like blackberries – everyone knew when you had been picking blackberries by the purple stain on your fingers and clothes.

Not edible but oh so much fun were the horse chestnuts or conkers. There was a row of six or more horse chestnut trees beside the road to Knotty Green. Such a delight when the green spiky and very unfriendly seed pods fell to the ground. The secret was inside. More round than the chestnuts we ate, conkers were the richest red/brown imaginable. If we had to prise them out of their soft covering, they felt moist to touch. Playing conkers is an age-old game and, for older boys especially, became very serious. My brothers soaked them in vinegar to harden them. A hole was bored right through and a piece of string threaded with a knot at one end to keep it in place. The idea was to bash your conker off someone else's and try and break it. Better than string was if they could use one of Dad's leather shoelaces.

Shoe repairs. My dad was no cobbler but in those lean times, shoes and boots were repaired rather than replaced. He had a cobbler's last made of very heavy iron with three feet of different sizes. The shoe needing a new sole or heel was placed over the appropriate foot of the last.

Dad had pieces of leather of different thickness. The piece needed was cut with a very sharp blade then small nails called brads hammered it onto the shoe or boot. Then came the dangerous task of trimming off any excess leather.

Heels were made of two or three layers of leather and the worn piece was taken off and a new piece hammered on. Dad's work boots also had extra metal tips put on the heels to minimise wear. It made his boots very noisy and I could always hear him walking on the cement path round the outside of the house. I loved to be able to help hammer in the brads and managed quite a few sore fingers when I hit them instead of the brads. I loved to polish the shoes too.

Particularly in winter when shoes were wet for months on end, keeping them protected with shoe polish wasn't the vanity of having shiny shoes. It was a task for doing in front of the fire, making sure there was no mud left on the shoes, then putting on the polish with one brush, allowing the polish to dry and then shining them with a softer brush. It was a wonderful sense of achievement to see them all lined up ready for morning. I suspect my brothers were happy to let me do theirs because I don't recall there ever being fights about who was going to polish the shoes.

And fights there were. Not great big arguments as such, but Geoff and I constantly needled each other, just squabbles that sorely tried Mother's patience. When I met Geoff in our early seventies, I asked him about that, and he said quite simply, 'You were a girl.' It never once occurred to me that my brothers didn't want me tagging along after them all the time when they were out in the woods, orchards and meadows. Plus I had to be included in playing darts, Ludo, Snakes and Ladders or Snap. I remember being very fed up when they joined the Boy Scouts. I was left behind.

There was no such thing as birthday parties but for as long as I can remember we had a wonderful time on bonfire night. A man called Guy Fawkes tried to blow up the Houses of Parliament on 5 November 1605 and the event was re-enacted in gardens all over Great Britain every year. It was a good excuse for Dad to get rid of rubbish and we built a large bonfire in the orchard just outside the garden. We bought fireworks from Marshalls in Beaconsfield. We all had our favourites. Mother loved Catherine wheels and Roman candles. I loved sparklers – writing my name in the air before they too quickly died – and of course rockets. My brothers loved bangers and jumping jacks. I think my dad loved them all. He took such care putting rockets into a milk bottle to be sure they soared unhindered into the night sky. My brothers set the jumping jacks loose and I climbed up on the fence to get away from them. I didn't like how unpredictable they were, which was probably most of the pleasure for my brothers. I also remember bangers being throw into the fire. I wonder now if they behaved differently from just being tossed at something or someone. After our small cache of fireworks were gone, large potatoes were put in the embers of the fire and we had potatoes in their jackets dripping with butter for supper.

At the far end of the village joining on to the Dip was a small private school for boys. They had the best fireworks, much bigger and brighter than our modest ones. We walked round to the Dip to watch them, along with many of our neighbours. It wasn't just children who enjoyed fireworks.

The next day, we all hunted for debris, a rocket that didn't perform properly, a banger that had been overlooked. They were considered treasures then.

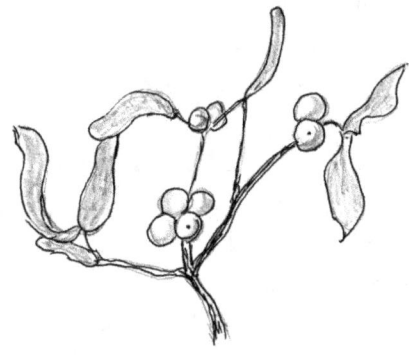

Mistletoe
Viscum album

After my birthday, winter never seemed far away and my world changed a lot. I had to cycle past Hogback Wood going to and from primary school. November fogs were the worst. They seemed to come down just before I left school. I paused at the top of the hill and could see nothing of Browns Farm at the bottom of the hill, no vestige of the railway line, and nothing of the woods beyond. I cycled quickly past Hogback Wood on foggy days. Everything was grey and dripping with mysterious rustlings coming from among the trees. I was convinced there was somebody there. We had the ghost of a Roman soldier living in the farmhouse, so it seemed perfectly logical to me that there was another in the wood.

The ghost in the farmhouse made itself known in different ways. When my parents first moved in, Mother was convinced someone was unhappy when the bed was placed near the top of the stairs. I never knew it in any other place but in the centre of a different wall. Mother also said she heard whistling as if someone was walking along the path outside and coming to the back door, but no one ever appeared.

I felt him at the top of the stairs behind my brothers' bedroom and the bathroom watching me go down. He wasn't an unfriendly presence as such but I didn't feel at ease especially if I was in the house alone, but no matter many times I turned I never actually saw him. Neither did my parents ever deny he was there.

But then there was Christmas. In those far-off days of make-do-and-mend, we only had presents on our birthdays and at Christmas. If we hungered for something, whether a penknife or a doll, then we knew we had to wait. I don't know when I stopped believing in Father Christmas. In fact, I don't even remember if I did believe in him.

In my last year at primary school, I was in the school pantomime – *Aladdin's Lamp*. I was in the chorus line and the first person to come out on stage. The pantomime was on in the evening and I remember my dad providing great bunches of holly and ivy to decorate the school hall, and Mother sitting in the front row watching.

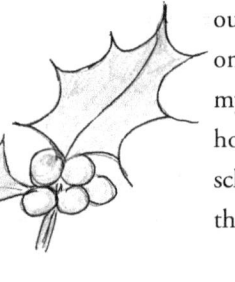
Holly
Aquifolioceae

In the weeks leading up to Christmas, all sorts of things happened and an air of secrecy pervaded the house. Just as my dad wasn't a cobbler, neither was he a carpenter, but I remember the things he made for us. I have already spoken of my doll's beds and cradles but Dad made things for my brothers. In the evenings, we had to play in the sitting room while Dad could be heard sawing and hammering in the kitchen. He made my brothers farm buildings and we carefully chose the animals and Matchbox series farm machinery to go with them.

He made them each a school-style desk to keep their treasures in. Steve went on a school excursion to the nearby Loudwater paper mill. He came home with bundles of offcuts which he kept in his desk. Oh, how I envied him that paper. I too went on a similar excursion but I didn't get the offcuts like he did.

Geoff collected birds' eggs. There was a very strict code to be adhered to. You only took one egg from a nest and disturbed it as little as possible. Geoff had been given a large shallow wooden box with a hinged lid. It was lined with sawdust and his precious eggs were kept inside. The insides of the eggs had to be carefully blown out by putting a small hole each end of the egg, no matter how small. If not done properly, you ended up with maggots. Ugh. I was taught how to do it, but I was never any good.

Apart from Mother and Dad making our gifts, there was extra cooking. Christmas cake: a heavy fruit cake which had to be covered in marzipan and that covered in royal icing. On Christmas Day, a frill of paper was put around the cake and there were small figures to be put on the top – a snowman, pine trees, children with a toboggan. Christmas pudding that was boiled in a piece of old bed sheeting. Coins were hidden in it, sixpences or threepenny bits, and whoever found one could keep it.

Christmas dinner. As children, we had school dinners which my parents paid for each Monday. I don't know how much they paid, but it must have been thought well worth it for their children to have a proper cooked dinner and pudding five days a week. It also meant they only had to provide a main meal at the weekends. We always had cereal and eggs for breakfast and often eggs for tea as well. Sunday roast of beef or lamb was traditional and I expect bought at a reduced rate as Dad's boss had a butcher's shop.

Christmas dinner was different. In late spring, my dad bought a dozen pullets – young hens that hadn't started laying. They were fattened up through the rest of the year and at Christmas he sold them to our neighbours for the extra money needed for our treats. He kept one for our Christmas dinner. Oh, what a treat. The big decision, to have the white meat from the breast, or the dark meat from a wing or part of a leg. I can also remember one year we had a goose and another time turkey. We had four turkeys Dad was fattening up for Christmas but oh, they were troublesome. For some reasons only known to turkeys, they liked to roost at night in the cherry tree branch that hung over the chicken pen. This made their breast meat tough and so not a good idea. I think the fox managed to eat a couple of them too. It was an experiment not repeated.

Christmas Eve was always a time of activity. My dad was paid weekly on Friday afternoon, hence the shopping on Saturday morning. In those days, workers were often paid a bonus called a Christmas box. It was a welcome addition to meagre funds for special things like Christmas crackers and small gifts to be placed on the tree, and nuts, oranges and sugar mice to be put at the bottom of Christmas stockings.

Our tree lived in the garden all year. On Christmas Eve, Dad dug it up and put it in a tin bucket and brought it indoors. Once placed in the corner of the sitting room – not too close to the fire – it was the task of the children to decorate the tree. First, red crêpe paper was wrapped around the bucket to hide it. Cotton wool was pretend snow to hide the dirt in the bucket. Tinsel came in long silver strands and was woven among the branches. Then came the delicate coloured balls. They were saved each year but inevitably one or two were broken and a few new ones had to be bought. They were supplemented by the bells I made from silver milk bottle tops. You had to take the tops off without tearing them, wash them carefully so they didn't smell and save them until Christmas. The tops were carefully pressed over the top of the lemon squeezer. A piece of cotton or embroidery thread was attached and they were hung on the tree. The very last thing to go on was the Christmas star, which went right at the very top. A few small gifts, one for each member of the family, were tucked close to the central trunk of the tree ready to be opened after Christmas lunch.

We made paperchains from specially purchased sheets of coloured paper cut into narrow strips. Mother made glue from flour and water – nowhere near as much fun as the glue at Sunday school. At some point, things changed and we bought packets of pre-cut strips that had glue at one end and just had to be licked. If you made the glue too wet, it didn't stick and suddenly during the day it would come unstuck and the whole string would come rustling down. Coloured crêpe paper was bought in rolls like hair ribbon and pinned from the corners of the room. The ceilings downstairs were very low in the farmhouse – a man six feet tall had to bend or hit his head on the beams. This meant that out streamers were best hung along the walls and only with great difficulty criss-crossing the room as the beams were so hard drawing pins would bend rather than go in.

Dad brought in bunches of holly and ivy, which was pinned in various places downstairs. The last thing he brought in was the mistletoe. He never said where he found it. There is a legend that says mistletoe has to be cut with a gold sickle, but I'm certain my dad didn't have one of those.

On Christmas Eve, Mother made mince pies and green ginger wine, which was served hot. The radio was always on for Christmas carols. Amongst the fruit stored in the pantry was a box of Cox's orange pippin apples. They had a distinctive flavour and a soft woolly texture and we always had them as part of our Christmas fare.

Christmas Day, we went to church. Like all children, I liked the carols and then it was walking home for Christmas dinner. It was the one day my dad helped wash up the dinner dishes. In the afternoons, we sat by the fire playing with new toys, eating nuts while getting the shells in the rugs. We listened to the Queen's Christmas message on the radio. There was absolute silence for those few minutes.

All was well unless there was a knock at the door because someone had left a gate open and the sheep or cows were out on the lane or the railway lines. No such thing as shrug that off; the situation had to be dealt with.

Snowdrops
Galanthus nivalis

Snow could happen anytime but not very often before Christmas. There was magic in the air to wake one morning and, as soon as I opened my eyes, I could tell by the bright light it had snowed during the night. Jack Frost would have made fantastic patterns in the ice on the window.

One morning, I went downstairs and opened the back door. I was faced with a wall of snow. The wind had blown it into a drift and we had to go out through the front door, find spades in the woodshed and dig a path from the back door to the chicken pen. The chickens looked startled when I opened the door of their shed and they paused before going down the plank of wood to the ground below. Snow had to be scraped off for them so they could get to the food trough and fresh water.

A bucket was kept near the back door for food scraps. Meal and warm water was added to this first thing in the morning and the mix fed to the chickens. When it had been snowing, it wasn't unusual to see the bucket overturned and footprints of fallow deer or rabbits, even a fox in the snow coming and going from the chicken bucket, though I never saw them.

Although all the other vegetables had been eaten from the garden, the Brussels sprouts were left. They looked so comical after it had snowed; each one had its little snow hat. I was happy enough to go out and pick some for 'a little bit of colour on the plate', as Mother used to say. They were so pretty as they sparkled with sunlight reflecting from the snow crystals, but oh how cold my fingers were – it was no use wearing gloves for this task.

All farm animals had to be fed when it snowed. Dad would take the tractor and trailer to the large mound of mangelwurzels. We had to help load them onto the trailer and hold tight as we were driven to the fields where the sheep or cattle were kept. Dad drove slowly around the field and we had to throw the mangelwurzels off. We also had to drop hay for them to eat, as there was little grass during winter. It was hard work and unheard of in today's world of safety precautions.

Snow didn't mean a day off school either. It just meant we had to walk instead of cycle. It was common for my dad to have to use the tractor to clear the roads out of the village so cars could come and go. The council trucks with salt to sprinkle didn't come out to us until much later in the day.

I was about seven years old when my cousin married, and I was one of her bridesmaids. It was bitterly cold and the other girl and I, who I had never met before, wore pale blue lightweight frocks with dainty white overlay and short puffy sleeves. Our headbands were pale blue velvet flowers and we each had a posy of white rosebuds with a red one in the centre. I can still remember standing outside the church between flurries of icy sleet having our photographs taken.

But there was much pleasure to be had in the snow. The Dip had a deep slope each side and a public footpath to take the short cut across the field. As soon as there was snow on the ground, toboggans or even old tin trays were found and children and adults from all around gathered to take advantage of the slippery slopes. There was a sort of unwritten law that each side take it in turns to minimise the number of crashes. The toboggans made the pathway lethal to walk on with the hard-packed ice, and walkers had to trudge through the deep soft snow on either side.

The beechwoods became a wonderland. Beech trees grow very tall and create a canopy high overhead that blocks out quite a lot of sunlight, so there is no undergrowth like bracken in a beechwood. This creates a wonderful haven in the hot weather, as it's always cool. When autumn winds have blown all the leaves off, that canopy becomes a delicate tracery of tiny twigs. When it snows, each of those tiny twigs has its own load of snow. As I walked among the trees, a slight breeze or a passing bird would knock the snow off with a soft thud. It was very cold if it happened to land on my head and trickle down my neck.

Winters seemed to have been one long struggle of being cold and wet. Coats, gloves and shoes all had to be put close to the fire overnight to try and dry the worst of the wetness out ready for morning. The memory of putting bare legs into damp wellington boots is something that can still make me shudder.

I would cycle home from school in the dark and stumble through the back door. Light and warmth immediately wrapped around me. Mother made the best beef stew. I hastily took off damp clothes and sat on the floor by the open fire. The house was quiet before my dad and brothers came home. This was when the sight and smell of those hyacinths was most appreciated. I watched the flames, the glowing embers and drifted – I know not where.

Outside in the garden, hidden under the climbing roses were not only lilies-of-the-valley but snowdrops. They were the first sign that spring was trying to throw off winter. They appeared before yellow and purple crocus, and long before daffodils, or violets. Their slender stems appeared among the snow and their petals etched with green were a wonder to behold...

Memories go on and on. They cross my mind unexpectedly, the sight of a flower, hearing a piece of music, or the name of scented soap from long ago. Post-war England was grim for so many but I had an enchanted childhood.

www.ingramcontent.com/pod-product-compliance
Lightning Source LLC
Chambersburg PA
CBHW062150100526
44589CB00014B/1768